WHAT THE CRITICS SAY:

W9-BIG-631

A very worthwhile addition to any travel library.
—**WCBS Newsradio**

Armed with these guides, you may never again stay in a conventional hotel.
—**Travelore Report**

Easily carried . . . neatly organized . . . wonderful. A helpful addition to my travel library. The authors wax as enthusiastically as I do about the almost too-quaint-to-believe Country Inns.
—**San Francisco Chronicle**

One can only welcome such guide books and wish them long, happy, and healthy lives in print.
—**Wichita Kansas Eagle**

This series of pocket-sized paperbacks will guide travelers to hundreds of little known and out of the way inns, lodges, and historic hotels. . . . a thorough menu.
—**(House Beautiful's) Colonial Homes**

Charming, extremely informative, clear and easy to read; excellent travelling companions.
—**Books-Across-The-Sea** *(The English Speaking Union)*

. . . a fine selection of inviting places to stay. . . provide excellent guidance. . . .
—**Blair & Ketchum's Country Journal**

Obviously designed for our kind of travel. . . . [the authors] have our kind of taste.
—**Daily Oklahoman**

The first guidebook was so successful that they have now taken on the whole nation. . . . Inns are chosen for charm, architectural style, location, furnishings and history.
—**Portland Oregonian**

Many quaint and comfy country inns throughout the United States. . . The authors have a grasp of history and legend.
—**Dallas (Tx.) News**

Very fine travel guides.
—**Santa Ana (Calif.) Register**

A wonderful source for planning trips.
—**Northampton (Mass.) Gazette**

. . . pocketsize books full of facts. . . . attractively made and illustrated.
—**New York Times Book Review**

Hundreds of lovely country inns reflecting the charm and hospitality of various areas throughout the U.S.
—**Youngstown (Ohio) Vindicator**

Some genius must have measured the average American dashboard, because the Compleat Traveler's Companions fit right between the tissues and bananas on our last trip. . . . These are good-looking books with good-looking photographs. . . . very useful.
—**East Hampton (N.Y.) Star**

ALSO AVAILABLE IN THE COMPLEAT TRAVELER SERIES

☐ *George Ferguson's* Europe by Eurail

☐ *George Ferguson's* Britain by Britrail

☐ *Fistell's* America by Train

☐ The Great American Guest House Book *(Bed & Breakfast U.S.A.)*

☐ Country Inns & Historic Hotels of Great Britain

☐ Country Inns & Historic Hotels of Canada

☐ Country Inns & Historic Hotels of Ireland

☐ Country New England Inns

☐ Country Inns & Historic Hotels of the Middle Atlantic States

☐ Country Inns & Historic Hotels of the South

☐ Country Inns & Historic Hotels of the Midwest & Rocky Mts.

☐ Country Inns & Historic Hotels of California and the West

☐ Guide to Country New England

☐ Guide to California and the Pacific Northwest

☐ Guide to Texas and the Southwest

☐ Guide to Virginia

☐ Guide to North Carolina

☐ Guide to Tennessee

If your local bookseller, gift shop, or country inn does not stock a particular title, ask them to order directly from Burt Franklin & Co., Inc., 235 East 44th Street, New York, New York 10017, U.S.A. Telephone orders are accepted from recognized retailers and credit card holders. In the United States, call, toll free, 1–800–223–0766 during regular business hours. (In New York State, call 212–687–5250.)

COUNTRY INNS

Lodges, and Historic Hotels of the

Middle Atlantic States

by

Anthony Hitchcock

and

Jean Lindgren

BURT FRANKLIN & CO.

Published by Burt Franklin & Company
235 East Forty-fourth Street
New York, New York 10017

Copyright ©1979, 1980, 1981, 1982, 1983 by Burt Franklin & Co., Inc.

FIFTH EDITION

Library of Congress Cataloging in Publication Data

Hitchcock, Anthony
Country inns, lodges, and historic
hotels of the Middle Atlantic States.

(The Compleat traveler's companion)
Rev. ed. of: Country inns, lodges, and historic
hotels of the Middle Atlantic States. c1982.
Includes index.
1. Hotels, taverns, etc. — Middle Atlantic States —
Directories.   I. Lindgren, Jean
II. Title   III. Series.
TX907.H539   1983   647'.947401   83–1424
ISBN 0–89102–271–6 (pbk.)

Cover illustration courtesy of
the Old Drovers Inn,
Dover Plains, New York

Manufactured in the United States of America

1 3 4 2

Contents

Introduction

AS WE EXPLORED the Middle Atlantic region, we discovered a wide range of wonderful accommodations. We luxuriated in old stone mills, fabulous brick Federal-style mansions, French *auberges*, and rustic Adirondack lodges. There truly are a wealth of places to go and sights to see within an easy drive of one of the most populous regions in the country. Mountain-lovers revel in the upper Adirondacks, the softer Catskills, and the resort-laden Poconos. Fishermen can fight the muskellunge (maximum legal weight: a whopping 35 pounds) and scrappy trout of northern waters or catch a striped bass in the surf off Long Island and top off their meal with fresh oysters from Bluepoint or the Chesapeake area. Skiers are constantly being lured away from Vermont and New Hampshire by slopes in New York and Pennsylvania.

No other region in the country is richer in history than these states. From the Pennsylvania battlefields to the historical museums and restored mansions of New York, from the fort at Ticonderoga to the seat of the navy at Annapolis, the region beckons millions of tourists each year. And if you come, the melting pot of America waits to greet you—be it the native Americans on regional reservations, the Pennsylvania Dutch of Lancaster County, the Irish, the English, the Swedes, the Italians, the black Americans, the Chinese, the Poles, or any other great ethnic group. The entire area is readily accessible, thanks to the excellent road system that interlaces these states.

We suggest that you write early for literature about the inns you have chosen as interesting. Read the brochures, look at the pictures, check the maps, and determine if the inns will actually meet your needs. Inns are not at all like motels. Each has its special qualities that may appeal to one person but not to another. Do not hesitate to call an innkeeper and discuss your requirements. In fact, it is our feeling that this is, for us, the most important thing to do before making a reservation. Country inns reflect the style and personality of the innkeeper. This personal ambience is more likely to affect your visit than in a motel or large hotel. Most innkeepers are highly understanding of the needs of their guests. If you are seeking, for example, an old-fashioned small country inn that is secluded from most outside distractions, ask before you go. We have purposely included a wide range of inns, lodges, small and historic hotels, and small resorts.

We have quoted the most recent room rates in a combined rate chart and index at the end of the book. Readers should note that the listed rates are *subject to change*. While the quoted rates are for double occupancy in most cases, single travelers as well as larger groups should inquire about special rates. We list daily room rates as based on the American Plan (AP, all three meals included), Modified American Plan (MAP, breakfast and dinner included), Bed and Breakfast (BB, either full or Continental breakfast included), or European Plan (EP, no meals). In many cases a tax and a service charge will be added. Be sure to ask. Children and pets present special problems for many inns. If either is *not* welcome at an inn it is noted in the description. These regulations also often change, and it is imperative that families traveling with either inquire in advance.

We suggest that before traveling to any state you write to its department of travel and tourism. Ask for the state road map and a packet of general travel information. If you have special travel interests or needs, the department can often send special pamphlets or hints. In the pages that follow, readers will discover that the material is organized by states. Within each state, listings are alphabetical by the names of the towns and villages. For those seeking a particular inn, there is an index at the end of the book, which also contains rate and credit-card information.

The inns discussed in this book were chosen for their inherent charm, based partially on their architectural style, location, furnishings, and history. We used no strict definition of an "inn" in selecting places for inclusion. Although the term usually denotes a place with both lodging and food, we have listed several that provide no meals. We find, in some cases, that the food operation actually is so dominant as to detract from the quiet and charm of a place. We did not include any of the old inns that only serve meals, although a great many exist in the region. The information incorporated here came from several sources: our personal knowledge of the inns, recommendations by others we deem reliable, and personal surveys of innkeepers. We have made every effort to provide information as carefully and accurately as possible, but we remind readers again that all rates and schedules are subject to change. Take particular note of any inn listed as open all year; many of these may close spontaneously during slow periods of the year for brief vacations. Once again: Call before going to any country inn. Finally, we have neither solicited nor accepted any fees or gratuities for inclusion of an inn in this book or in any other book in the Compleat Traveler series.

We hope this book will continue to grow in usefulness in successive editions. For this reason, we are eager to learn of your experiences at the inns listed in this volume and to receive your suggestions for additions or deletions for future volumes. We will make every effort to answer all letters personally. Please write to us in care of our publishers: Burt Franklin & Co., 235 East Forty-fourth Street, New York, NY 10017.

Have a good trip!

JEAN LINDGREN
ANTHONY HITCHCOCK

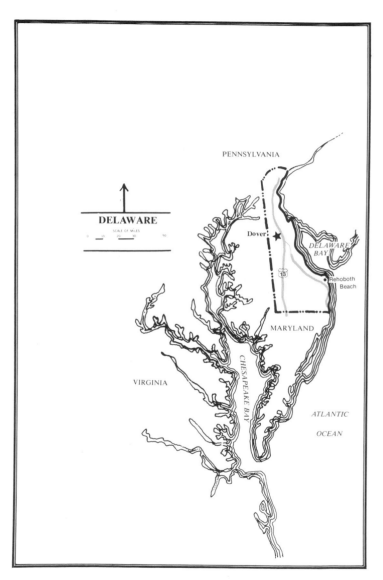

Delaware

New Castle, Delaware

WILLIAM PENN GUEST HOUSE

206 Delaware Street, New Castle, DE 19720. 302-328-7736. *Innkeepers:* Mr. and Mrs. Richard Burwell. Open all year.

When William Penn first landed in New Castle in 1682, he walked only a few hundred feet to the home of Arnoldus de LaGrange, who was his host and a witness to the "turf and twig" ceremony by which Penn took possession of his New World territory. At the time, LaGrange's home was a year old. It has grown a bit in three centuries, but continues to receive overnight guests who come to see the state's best-preserved prerevolutionary town.

Named for its most famous overnight guest, the William Penn House is operated by its congenial owners, Mr. and Mrs. Richard Burwell, who used to live next door. Mrs. Burwell bought the historic house as a "surprise" one day about twenty years ago when her husband was away. After recovering from his "surprise," he and his wife set out to restore the William Penn's rooms. The result is four comfortable guest rooms (including the one Penn slept in) upstairs and a gracious living room and kitchen below. Although many guests choose the Penn quarters, our favorite room is upstairs, tucked under the eaves and a dormer window.

Accommodations: 4 rooms with shared baths. *Pets:* Not permitted. *Driving Instructions:* From I-295, take Route 9 into New Castle. Route 9 eventually becomes Delaware Street.

Rehoboth Beach, Delaware

THE CORNER CUPBOARD INN

50 Park Avenue, Rehoboth Beach, DE 19971. 302-227-8553. *Innkeeper:* Elizabeth Gundry Hooper. Inn and restaurant open Memorial Day weekend through September. Inn open the rest of the year for lodgings only, with advance reservations.

The Corner Cupboard was built as a private home for Elizabeth Hooper's aunt and uncle in 1927. Five years later, to get through the Depression era, they began to operate the home as an inn. Elizabeth helped out here as a teen-ager and returned in 1974 to buy the place from her aunt. The inn is a litttle house nestled under tall pines on a peaceful side road of sand. The roar of the surf can be heard above the winds in the pines. The house is just behind a stand of holly trees. The unpaved road is divided down the center by a grove of trees secluding the inn from the residential homes surrounding it. Entry — through the inn's living room, an inviting setting without a front desk or other typical hotel paraphernalia — is like stepping into a home. In winter this room is carpeted with Oriental and braided rugs, and upholstered chairs are grouped about the fire in the brick hearth.

Surprisingly, the inn has quite a few guest rooms. Its appearance makes it seem much smaller and more intimate than it actually is. The rooms, all different, are attractively decorated with a variety of antiques and more modern furniture collected over the years. Most of them are upstairs off the wide hallway that displays a collection of old baskets on its walls. A back bedroom features wallpaper printed with tiny flowers and has a four-poster double bed. Four small guest rooms in back of the main house, off the brick courtyard, are furnished simply.

Downstairs, below the sleeping porch, is a solarium that is quite snug in winter. A Franklin stove adds warmth to this plant-filled room where the television resides. In summer the room is opened up, the stove is put away, and tables are set out so that guests can enjoy their breakfast there. The inn is renowned for this meal, which features kidney stew and grits, creamed chicken on waffles, or local country sausage or scrapple. The dining room, just off the solarium, is on a large screened-in side porch decorated with many hanging flowering plants and cooled by paddle fans. In warm months dinner is served out here by candlelight. Specials include fresh seafoods, roast lamb, liver with bacon or onions, sweetbreads with ham, broiled lobster, and the region's famous Chesapeake crabs. All baking is done in the inn's big kitchen, and guests reap the benefits with baskets of hot rolls and dessert pastries.

The beach is a block and a half from the inn down a sandy lane. The boardwalk and town are also within walking distance. Elizabeth can steer interested guests to good antiquing and sightseeing spots in the area. This is a friendly little inn with an equally friendly innkeeper.

Accommodations: 14 rooms, 9 with private bath. *Pets:* Permitted in some rooms. *Driving Instructions:* Take Route 14 from Wilmington to the Rehoboth turnoff. Soon after the turnoff, take a left beyond the lighthouse and then an immediate right on Columbia. Take Columbia to Second Street, and drive one block to Park Avenue. Turn left on Park to the inn. If time permits, write the inn for a map of Rehoboth Beach. Park Avenue exists in bits and pieces throughout the village, and the inn may be a little hard to find on the first visit.

District of Columbia

Washington, D.C.

KALORAMA GUEST HOUSE

1854 Mintwood Place, N.W., Washington, D.C. 20009. 202-667-6389. *Innkeeper:* Jim Mench. Open all year.

Kalorama Guest House is a welcome oasis of Victorian gentility in the nation's bustling capital. Centrally located in the Kalorama Triangle area in downtown Washington, D.C., the guest house is just minutes from the Capitol, the White House, and the famous museums and monuments on the Mall. The Kalorama, built around 1880, retains many of its original features, such as the striking chandelier and fireplace in the parlor.

The inn has been decorated and refurbished to assure guests of a truly Victorian bed-and-breakfast experience in the best European tradition. The parlor sets the mood with its nineteenth-century Empire couches and period artwork. Sherry is served by the fireside in the late afternoon, and the Continental breakfast is set out here each morning.

Each guest room has a brass headboard, a plush comforter, and matching pillow shams and drapes. There are wing chairs, Oriental area rugs on polished hardwood floors, pots of greenery, and occa-

sionally fresh flowers in the rooms. Three guest rooms have nonworking fireplaces,

Accommodations: 6 rooms with shared bath. *Pets:* Not permitted. *Driving Instructions:* The Kalorama Triangle is formed by Connecticut Avenue, Calvert Street, and Columbia Road, just below the National Zoological Garden and Rock Creek Park.

PENNSYLVANIA

Grantsville

Woodsboro

Frederick
New Market
Buckeystown

Chestertown

DELAWARE BAY

Potomac River

Annapolis

Greensboro
Easton
Oxford
St. Michaels

DELAWARE

J.F. KENNEDY MEM. HY.

CHESAPEAKE BAY

VIRGINIA

Potomac River

Princess Anne

ATLANTIC OCEAN

MARYLAND

SCALE OF MILES
0   10   20   30   50

Maryland

Annapolis, Maryland

Founded in the mid-seventeenth century, Annapolis was the first peacetime capital of the United States. Since 1845 it has been the home of the *United States Naval Academy* as well as the third oldest college in the country, *Saint John's College*, founded in 1696. Visitors planning a thorough tour of the city should obtain a copy of "Rambling thru Annapolis," by Barbara Butt. It is available from the Chamber of Commerce at 171 Conduit Street. Call 301-268-7676. Sites in the city open to the public include the *Maryland State House* (1779), the *Old Treasury Building*, the *Hammond-Harwood House,* the *Paca House and Gardens*, the *Naval Academy Museum*, and the *crypt of Captain John Paul Jones*. The *City Dock* area with the restored *City Market*, restaurants, and shops is an interesting stop. The *Naval Historical Wax Museum* tells the story of two hundred years of naval history, from John Paul Jones to John F. Kennedy of *PT-109*.

MARYLAND INN

Church Circle, Annapolis, MD 21401. 301-263-2641. *Innkeeper:* Peg Bednarsky. Open all year.

Late in the seventeenth century the town fathers of Annapolis set aside a centrally located plot of land on Church Circle for the use of the town drummer, who was to this capital city what the town crier was to other contemporary cities. In 1772, after the demise of the drummer as an important figure, Thomas Hyde of Severn built the first part of the now historic Maryland Inn. His advertisement in the January 31, 1782, *Maryland Gazette* read, "Elegant brick house adjoining Church Circle in a dry and healthy part of the city . . . 22 rooms, 20 fireplaces, 2 kitchens . . . one of the first houses in the State

for a house of entertainment." The original part of the inn still stands, its wedge shape dominating the circle a block from the State House and the Governor's Mansion and across the street from Saint Anne's Church. The inn is surrounded by dozens of restored pre-1800 buildings, which have made Annapolis almost as popular as Williamsburg among historically minded travelers. Approximately a hundred years after Hyde erected his inn, the roof was raised and a fourth floor added. At this time the Victorian porches were also added to the wedge-shaped building.

Today, the Maryland Inn continues the tradition of two centuries of innkeeping. It has managed to preserve its personal touches despite growing to comprise more than forty guest rooms. Throughout the inn the fine walnut banisters, paneling, and other woodwork, as well as the many original fireplaces, have been preserved. Modern amenities intermingle with the many examples of colonial craftsmanship. Rooms have tiled private bathrooms, telephones, television, and air conditioning. Their comfort is attested to by many members of the Maryland legislature staying at the Maryland Inn through the legislative sessions each year. Each room is furnished with a nice selection of period antiques. Beds bear reproductions of Queen Elizabeth–style white spreads, and most rooms have a writing desk. The attractive Hyde Suite retains many of its original features such as the woodwork, mantel, and cornices. The suite has fireplaces in both the bedroom and the sitting room, Oriental rugs on the floor, and its own kitchen. It is particularly private, accessible only from the veranda on the second floor.

The Treaty of Paris Room, named in honor of the pact that ended the War of Independence (signed in the Annapolis State House, minutes away), combines the warmth of old brick and heavy wood beams with a fire in a wide fireplace that has had similar fires going for more than two hundred years. The luncheon menu offers salads, sandwiches (the Wye Island combines one of the inn's famed crab cakes with a toasted roll), and several hot luncheon dishes. In the evening, candlelight adds an even more romantic touch to the room. Offerings with a Continental flair include a mixture of Chesapeake Bay seafood specialties, steaks and roasts, and several veal dishes. Veal Alexandra combines mushrooms, spinach, Smithfield ham, and mozzarella cheese with veal scallops; the Treaty of Paris is a blend of local and imported seafoods covered with a wine sauce and served in pastry puffs.

The adjoining King of France Tavern was opened in 1784. Twentieth-century offerings there include fine jazz performances by such musicians as Charlie Byrd, Earl "Fatha" Hines, and Ethel Ennis. The tavern's original stone walls, exposed wooden beams, and brick chimneys and arches are characteristic of the eighteenth century.

Accommodations: 44 rooms with private bath. *Driving Instructions:* Take Main Street in Annapolis to Church Circle (the intersection of West, College, Main, and Duke of Gloucester streets).

Buckeystown, Maryland

THE INN AT BUCKEYSTOWN

3521 Buckeystown Pike, Buckeystown, MD 21717. 301-874-5755.
Innkeepers: M. G. Martinez and D. R. Pelz. Open all year.

In the heart of Buckeystown, a historic eighteenth-century village on the Monocacy River, stands a Victorian mansion built in the 1890s. The estate sits on 2½ acres of manicured lawns and shrubs, surrounded by chestnut and dogwood trees. Its owners, innkeepers Martinez and Pelz, restored the house and opened it to guests for "bed and board" in 1982. The black-shuttered house, with its wraparound porches and tidy dental moldings, was given a fresh coat of paint inside and out. The floors were polished until they gleamed, and rooms were furnished with a blend of Victorian period pieces and modern upholstered couches and chairs. The public rooms have ornate crystal chandeliers, and three rooms have working fireplaces.

A golden oak–paneled staircase leads to the guest rooms above. Each room features welcoming carafes of port, perhaps a bowl of fruit, and a selection of the latest books and magazines, and furnishings share the limelight with such thoughtful creature comforts as electric blankets and air conditioning.

Meals are served on period Victorian silver, china, and crystal in the inn's spacious dining room. The cuisine is eclectic, emphasizing classic French cooking and the frequent use of veal. Nonetheless, the meal of the evening may also be a traditional "down-home" Southern feast or a Pennsylvania Dutch or Basque dinner. The innkeepers include complimentary wines with the meals, and guests are free to bring their own hard liquor. Dinner one fall evening featured pâté maison, cream of Jack-o'-lantern soup, and avocado and grapefruit salad. The entrée was veal in wine and mushroom sauce accompanied by pasta shells, broccoli, sourdough French bread and followed by deep-dish apple cobbler with cream.

An English sheepdog named Amos will gladly join guests for a stroll of the grounds, including a stop at Civil War era graveyard. Amos is also happy to curl up sociably by the hearth while guests enjoy a good book or chat together.

Buckeystown is less than an hour from Washington and Baltimore and a short drive from Gettysburg, Harpers Ferry, and New Market, Maryland's prime antiquing district.

Accommodations: 5 rooms with shared baths. *Pets and Children:* Not permitted. *Driving Instructions:* The inn is 5 miles south of Frederick, on Route 85.

Chestertown, Maryland

THE INN AT MITCHELL HOUSE

Route 21, Chestertown, Maryland. *Mailing address:* Box 329,
R.D. 2, Tolchester Estates, Chestertown, MD 21620. 301-
778-6500. *Innkeepers:* Dorris and Al Marshall. Open all year.

The 1,000 acres that once constituted this eighteenth-century farm
have been reduced over the years to 10 acres of rolling pasture, lawns,
woodlands, a stream, and a farm pond complete with geese, swans, a
red fox, and deer. The Williamsburg-style colonial structure now
known as The Inn at Mitchell House was built in two sections—the
east wing in 1743 and the west in 1825. Today, Mitchell House sits on
a grassy knoll at the end of a tree-lined half-mile driveway.

The manor house was converted to an inn by the Marshalls in 1982.
They have decorated its rooms in Williamsburg colors and filled them
with antiques spanning the decades of the estate's existence. They
offer antiques for sale at their Pit and Pendulum Antique Shop, and a
collection of primitives at what was once the estate's smokehouse.

Thoughtfully set out in the antique-filled guest rooms are fresh
flowers, fruit, and complimentary wine. Designer sheets and over-
sized towels are an additional touch of luxury. All but one of the guest

rooms have working fireplaces, and two feature sitting rooms as well.

A full country breakfast is served with all the fixings including homemade muffins and often grits or Chestertown scrapple. The dining room has a handsome harvest table as well as several smaller tavern tables used for breakfast. Many guests enjoy playing chess or cards in the parlor. While you are at the inn, be sure to ask about Sir Peter Parker (one of the guest rooms is named for him). He had a rather unusual trip from the Mitchell House back to his native England.

Accommodations: 5 rooms with shared baths. *Pets and Children:* Not permitted. *Driving Instructions:* From Chestertown, take Route 20 west 7 miles to Route 21. Turn right and drive 3 miles to the inn.

WHITE SWAN TAVERN

231 High Street, Chestertown, MD 21620. 301-778-2300. *Innkeeper:* Mary S. Clarkson. Open all year.

Tranquil Chestertown, on Maryland's Eastern Shore, was, in the eighteenth century, an active seaport and a focus of trade between Britain, the colonies, and the West Indies. Many Georgian and Federal homes built during that period by wealthy merchants still stand in this pretty village. One such home, now the White Swan Tavern, had a somewhat more humble beginning. Its origin was as a 1795 one-room dwelling for a shoemaker. The one room survived and is, today, the John Lovegrove Kitchen, one of the superbly restored guest rooms in the inn. This room, with its exposed beams, brick floor, and wide country-kitchen fireplace, has a number of early antique pieces, as well as modern beds.

Other parts of the White Swan date from 1733 and 1795. Of the remaining rooms, all but one are decorated with antiques and reproduction furniture of the colonial period, with four-posters and canopied beds the rule. The other, in the T. W. Elliason Suite, is the innkeeper's valentine to the Victorian period. Here marble-topped tables, tufted couches, and high-backed Victorian beds are set off by the bold colors of the period.

Each of the inn's four public rooms has been carefully researched and decorated and furnished in the manner of the eighteenth century. The Nicholson Room serves as a formal drawing room. It is furnished in a purposefully austere and dignified manner typical of rooms owned by Chestertown's wealthier merchants. Somewhat more casual

is the King Joseph Room, a sitting room reserved for guests and their friends. Here the inn's television set resides, tables are provided for postcard writing, and upholstered chairs invite guests to relax and read.

Tea is served daily in the Isaac Cannell Room every afternoon to both guests and the public. This room was the original tavern room during the first half of the nineteenth century, when it was called by many the "best tavern in town." It is also the place where Continental breakfast is served to guests each morning.

The White Swan has gone to some length to cater to the comfort of its guests, not only in the furnishings of the rooms but also in those myriad little attentions that set apart a true country inn from hotels or motels. Apart from this, the White Swan's meticulous restoration sets it apart from most other small inns we know.

Accommodations: 5 rooms with private bath. *Pets:* Not permitted. *Driving Instructions:* Chestertown is on Route 213, off Route 301, on Maryland's Eastern Shore.

Easton, Maryland

THE TIDEWATER INN

Dover and Harrison streets, Easton, MD 21601. 301-822-1300.

Innkeeper: Anton J. Hoevenaars. Open all year.

The Tidewater Inn is not, in truth, a historic old country inn. It was built in this century, but its classic lines and fine detailing inside and out are not likely to reveal its recent heritage. Its brick exterior blends perfectly into the colonial and Federal architecture of this dignified Maryland town.

The inn's carefully selected interior appointments are evident as soon as one enters the lobby. Velvet and brocade chairs are drawn up to the fireplace at one side of the room, opposite the reception desk. Arched doorways lead to the inn's gift shops, as well as to several dining rooms. Dominating the lobby is a spiral staircase curving to the upper floors. A second sitting area, tucked under the curve of the stairs, has crewel-work upholstered wing chairs—a comfortable and quiet spot where guests can read. The main dining room's floor-to-ceiling windows overlook the swimming pool. The dining room is decorated in reds and white, and a red and white paneled fireplace stands at one end. The extensive dinner menu here draws heavily on local seafood. Eastern Shore entrées include crab Imperial, crab cakes, and soft-shell crabs, as well as crab and shrimp Norfolk and broiled rockfish. Ten or so meat and poultry selections with a Continental touch include filet mignon with béarnaise sauce, and chateaubriand bouquetière. A special gourmet menu is also available on twenty-four hours' notice. Some of its offerings are roast pheasant, fillet of beef Wellington, and diamondback terrapin. There is a second, less formal dining area at the inn, and breakfast and luncheon are also available daily.

The guest rooms range from a few small singles to fully appointed suites of three to five rooms. All have air conditioning, color television, and comfortable traditional hotel furnishings. Ice machines are available on all floors, and a soda machine is on the fourth floor. The inn makes a special effort to cater to hunters drawn by the Eastern Shore's long and excellent waterfowl season. Hunters planning to stay at the Tidewater during the season must make reservations early.

Accommodations: 120 rooms with private bath. *Driving Instructions:* From Easton take Route 50 to Dover Street (Route 331), go west on Route 331 for 7 blocks to Harrison Street. The inn is on the corner of Dover and Harrison.

SPRING BANK FARM INN

Harmony Grove, 7945 Worman's Mill Road, Frederick, MD 21701. 301-694-0440. *Innkeepers:* Beverly and Ray Compton. Open all year.

In his 1882 *History of Western Maryland,* Thomas Scharf described the home of George Houck as containing "all the modern improvements that judiciously-expended wealth could obtain or refined taste suggest." In 1880, George Houck built his sixteen-room brick Italianate house just on the outskirts of Frederick, in the small community of Harmony Grove. In 1980, Beverly and Ray Compton bought the historic structure and set about restoring it as an inn.

Guest rooms at Spring Bank Farm are spacious, with 12-foot ceilings, plaster moldings, 9-foot windows, and heart-pine floors. The stenciled ceilings are a particularly fine feature of this house. When the restoration has been completed, guest rooms are expected to total eight. As the completed ones do now, each room will contain antique furniture and period linens.

Guests at the inn are welcome to share the Compton's library containing books on Maryland history, gardening, aviation, and antiques. The elegant double parlor has bay-window seats, a marbelized fireplace, Oriental rugs, warm brass decorations, and Victorian furniture. Doors to the foyer each contain panels of copper-wheel etched glass.

Spring Bank Farm has been particularly popular with honeymooning couples, but everyone who stays here enjoys antiquing, driving over the wooded country roads, and exploring nearby Harpers Ferry and Gettysburg, both less than an hour's drive away.

Accommodations: 3 (presently), 1 with private bath. *Pets and children:* Not permitted. *Driving Instructions:* The inn is 3 miles north of Frederick, on Route 355.

Grantsville, Maryland

THE CASSELMAN INN

Main Street, Grantsville, MD 21536. 301-895-5055 or 5266. *Innkeepers:* Mr. and Mrs. Ivan J. Miller. Open all year.

Maryland is a state of many surprises, one being that its western townships are more than 250 miles from the Atlantic Coast. Along historic Route 40, in the mountainous region near Cumberland, are the village of Grantsville and its Casselman Inn. Settled by Amish Mennonites in the early nineteenth century, the town was an important stopping point on the road west. In 1824 one Solomon Sterner built a brick two-story tavern. The bricks he used were handmade and fired on the tavern's land, and the woodwork was hand-hewn and hand planed nearby. Of particular note is the handsome cherry rail ascending to the third floor. Most of The Casselman's guest rooms are in a recently constructed motel building adjacent to the inn, although there are several antique-furnished ones upstairs in the original building.

The inn's restaurant serves three meals a day to guests and the public; dinner offerings include — in addition to such familiar items as honey-dipped chicken, beef tenderloin, and breaded haddock — Amish specialties, grilled cured ham, and even breaded beef brain. For dessert Mrs. Miller prepares a variety of pies.

Accommodations: 45 rooms, 42 with private bath. *Pets:* Not permitted. *Driving Instructions:* The inn is on Route 40, just north of the Grantsville exit off I-48.

Greensboro, Maryland

Greensboro, a quiet pre-Revolutionary farm town in the center of Maryland's Eastern Shore, is surrounded by fields of corn and grazing animals. The village has been experiencing a gradual rebirth since the reopening of the Riverside Hotel, which had been closed for twenty-five years, and the restoration of several old Victorian gingerbread homes on Main Street.

RIVERSIDE HOTEL

North Main Street, Greensboro, Maryland. Mailing address: P.O. Box 179, Greensboro, MD 21639. 301-482-8382 or 301-482-6301. *Innkeepers:* Joseph and Joan Olevsky. Open all year. Restaurant open all week in season and Thursday through Sunday December 1 to Easter.

The Riverside Hotel, at curbside, is a classic turn-of-the-century, flat-front hotel with a long, low porch bearing pots of flowers and creaky rockers and porch swings. Inside, guests soon learn what those bypassed places from the old days really used to look like; this is it. The Riverside and its decor are results of years of restoration.

The guest rooms are on the second floor, a repository for antiques, memorabilia, and collectibles. In the hallway are cupboards and marble-topped tables filled with china, dolls, and even a stuffed pheasant or two. The overall effect is that of ornate Victoriana typified by lamps with silk shades, overstuffed Art Deco chairs, knickknacks, and large mirrors.

Each guest room has its own decor and personality. There are floral-print wallpapers, Victorian curlicue papers, Jenny Lind spool beds and heavy brass, oak, and walnut beds. Four bathrooms serve these rooms, two with deep claw-footed tubs and two with more modern tub showers.

The gardens around the hotel are filled with many kinds of flowers and unusual bushes and ornamental trees. A bonsai garden has been worked into the terraced steps that descend to the river behind the hotel.

Accommodations: 16 rooms sharing 4 hall baths. *Pets:* Permitted if well behaved and arrangements made in advance. *Driving Instructions:* From Washington or Baltimore, take the Bay Bridge (Route 50) heading east. Turn left onto Route 404 and left again onto Route 480, Greensboro's Main Street.

THE STRAWBERRY INN

17 Main Street, New Market, MD. Mailing address: Box 237, New Market, MD 21774. 301-865-3318. *Innkeepers*: Jane and Ed Rossig. Open all year.

Main Street, where the Strawberry Inn is situated, was once part of the historic National Pike of Frederick County, where the six-horse Conestoga wagons rumbled by on their way to the Ohio frontier. The inn, built in the mid-nineteenth century, is a small white clapboard Victorian house with black shutters and a front porch flanked by old boxwoods. Every little dream house should have a classic white picket fence like the one that encloses the Strawberry Inn's tree-shaded yards.

The Rossigs are house restorers par excellence, as their restoration of this inn demonstrates. The rooms, with their old wide-plank floors, were stripped of layers of old wallpapers and paint and refurbished with lovely reproduction papers accented with fresh paint. The ceiling moldings of the downstairs rooms, carefully repaired and painted, are ornately decorative borders bearing a lower trim that resembles a jack-o'-lantern's teeth; for this reason, they are called "dental moldings." The dining room, the most recent restoration, is bright and attractive, with fancy gold wallpaper complete with peacocks. This paper is a copy of some that was hung in the mansion of Massachusetts's first governor. The room's bay window overlooks the many adjoining backyards of this antique little town. Guests may choose to have their breakfast here at the hunt-table buffet or enjoy the luxury of breakfast in bed. The Rossigs place butler's trays of juice, hot buns, and coffee, tea, or hot chocolate outside guests' doors at an hour specified by the guest.

The hall has beautiful original hand stenciling at the baseboards and near the ceiling. Their discovery came as a pleasant surprise at the end of a long day of stripping ugly old wallpaper. The stencils needed minor touch-ups but were mostly in fine condition. The Rossigs quickly put away the planned new wallpaper for that area of the house, but every last one of the guest-room ceilings had to be replaced, thanks to gravity and the march of time.

Downstairs rooms consist of a Victorian living room furnished with the Rossigs' period antiques. The room is a comfortable place to sit and relax in front of a fire in the old fireplace. Both this room and the parlor across the hall have the original walnut interior shutters, and the upper window section is of ornately etched frosted glass. The former parlor is now the largest of the guest rooms. It is spacious enough to include a sitting area. Guests in this and the upper rooms enjoy Victorian surroundings complete with antique brass beds, antique spreads, and old walnut dressers, and where necessary, artful period reproductions are blended into the décor. All the rooms have modern tiled private baths.

As the inn serves only breakfast, the Rossigs will recommend nearby restaurants. Two that they particularly like are Mrs. Mealey's, in one of the town's old taverns, and the village tearoom, down the street.

Accommodations: 4 rooms with private bath. *Pets:* Not permitted. *Children:* Under eight not permitted. *Driving Instructions:* From Frederick, Maryland, take I-70 East approximately 7 miles to exit 60. Follow signs to New Market, which is about a mile from the exit.

Oxford is a historic city that predated Baltimore in its development and once ranked in importance as a port with Annapolis. It is an important boat-building and fishing village today. The *Oxford Town Museum* adjoining the town hall is open Friday through Sunday from 2 to 5. The *Tred Avon Ferry*, thought to be the oldest noncable ferry in the country, conveys today's passengers on modern diesel-powered boats that offer short, scenic rides across the mouth of the Tred Avon River. The *Customs House* at Morris and the Strand is a replica of the first customs house that occupied this site shortly after the Revolutionary War.

ROBERT MORRIS INN

On the Tred Avon, Oxford, MD 21654. 301-226-5111. *Innkeepers:* Ken and Wendy Gibson. Open all year except Christmas week.
When we pulled up to the Robert Morris Inn one drizzly afternoon, we knew that we had come to a special place. Even in January the grounds surrounding the 1710 mansard-roofed boyhood home of Robert Morris, Jr., were in perfect repair. Passing under the columned porch that runs the entire length of the inn's front, one enters through centuries-old pine doors into a center hall. Off to the left is a formal sitting room with a tall grandfather clock and paneling painted a shade of Williamsburg blue that sets off the antique furniture.

Across the hall are the dining rooms, which descend in formality as one goes from the hall to the side of the building. The first has a pair of jeweled chandeliers that set the tone in a room where formal dress is the rule. To the rear are the Tap Room and the Tavern. The small Tap Room has floor-to-ceiling, random-width dark paneling, a beamed ceiling, and a 6-foot-wide fireplace, which had a fire going both times we had breakfast here. The inn's dinner choices indicate its owners' passion for the seafood of the Chesapeake Bay region.

The Robert Morris has been restored in such a way that it almost appears not to be a restoration. Rather, guests feel as if they were staying at the Morris house two hundred years ago. Ships' carpenters built the house well: The original staircase is intact, as are the old wide-board pine floors. One corner room has walls reflecting the lines

of the mansard roof, pierced by two dormers with views of the river below. Its tall four-poster bed has been provided with a diminutive set of steps for easier access. In one corner of the room, a century-old trundle bed is next to a reproduction of an early swinging cradle.

The Robert Morris has chosen a graceful way of growing with its success. Instead of adding on to the old building (the exception being the recently added brick and slate tavern), the innkeepers simply bought and renovated other buildings within sight of the original.

The Robert Morris is a truly historic inn. Part of it was sixty-five years old at the time of the Revolution, a war partially financed by Morris himself, who risked all of his savings to support his belief in the newly formed United States.

Accommodations: 34 rooms, plus a cottage and an apartment; about two-thirds with private or connecting bath. *Pets:* Not permitted. *Driving Instructions:* Take Route 50 to Easton, then Route 333 to Oxford. Drive through town to the river's edge and the inn. The inn is also reached by boat from Chesapeake Bay to the Choptank River to the Tred Avon.

THE WASHINGTON HOTEL AND INN

Somerset Avenue, Princess Anne, MD 21853. 301-651-2525. *Innkeeper*: Mrs. Robert Murphey. Open all year.

This old hotel, in the center of historic Princess Anne, with its eighteenth-century homes, has been in the Murphey family for nearly fifty years. Built in 1744, the inn still sports a wide double staircase designed for the hoop-skirted ladies of that period. Both the Washington Hotel and the nearby Teackle Mansion were settings of George Alfred Townsend's novel *The Entailed Hat*. The dining room retains many of the original features such as an unusual paneled ceiling, an enormous corner cupboard and sideboard, and a large fireplace with its iron crane and big black pot still attached. The dining room is open to guests and the public for all meals. Mrs. Murphey's son Robert manages the restaurant, which features Chesapeake Bay's famous oysters, crabs, and other fresh seafood dishes. The lobby is filled with pictures, including one of each of the U.S. presidents. The rooms are furnished with old furniture and all have air conditioning and television.

Accommodations: 16 rooms, 8 with private bath. *Pets:* Not permitted. *Driving Instructions:* The hotel is in Maryland's eastern section, on the Chesapeake Bay side. Take Route 13 south from Salisbury and turn off into the town of Princess Anne.

THE INN AT PERRY CABIN

Talbot Street, St. Michaels, Maryland. *Mailing address:* Box 247, St. Michaels, MD 21663. 301-745-5178. *Innkeepers:* The Meyerhoff family. Open all year.

This grand old estate stands on the banks of the Miles River on Maryland's Eastern Shore and overlooks broad lawns sweeping down to Fogg Cove. The inn was built in the early nineteenth century by Samuel Hambleton, a purser in the U.S. Navy who served under Commodore Oliver Hazard Perry during the War of 1812. Hambleton so admired Perry that he named his home in his honor. After a century as a private home, Perry Cabin was turned into an inn and later became a riding academy. The Meyerhoff family completely refurbished the estate, adding a new kitchen wing in keeping with the architecture of the estate's original carriage house. The Carriage House is now the home of the Spectacular Bid Bar, with its dark wood trim, Tiffany-style lamps, and deep blue walls. The Meyerhoffs own the Thoroughbred Spectacular Bid and have decorated the bar with racing memorabilia.

The picture windows of the inn's three dining rooms look out on the river and cove. Specialties of the house include Maryland seafood dishes such as crab cakes and fried Chesapeake Bay oysters, as well as rack of baby lamb and steak au poivre. In warm weather, cocktails are served in a gazebo bar on the terrace.

The restored rooms throughout the inn are furnished with family antiques; great care has been taken in the preservation of the paneled fireplaces, arched doorways, and original doors. A curving carpeted staircase leads to the guest rooms, each decorated with wallcoverings and fabrics in keeping with the formal antique furnishings of Perry Cabin.

Complimentary breakfasts of sweet rolls and coffee are served to guests, and box lunches may be ordered for the next day's explorations of the scenic Eastern Shore. The Meyerhoffs thoughtfully provide bicycles for use by guests, which is particularly helpful for those who arrive at Perry Cabin by boat.

Accommodations: 6 rooms with private bath. *Pets:* Not permitted. *Driving Instructions:* St. Michaels is on Route 33, west of Easton.

SMITHTON

412 South Talbot Street, St. Michaels, Maryland. *Mailing address:* Box 638, St. Michaels, MD 21663. 301-745-5793. *Innkeeper:* Allan Smith. Open all year.

In 1812 the people of St. Michaels had to defend their town from a British attack. The important ship-building town was defended by its local militia under the command of Colonel Joseph Kemp, a shipyard owner whose new home on Main Street would also have been lost if the British had been victorious. The defense was successful, and today Colonel Kemp's fine brick home is the Smithton Inn, welcoming guests to a perfectly re-created atmosphere of late-eighteenth-century Maryland.

At Smithton guests find fresh flowers in all rooms, working fireplaces in four, and four-poster rope beds, trundle beds, feather beds, washstands with running water, handmade quilts in winter and air conditioning in summer, down pillows, and night shirts for guests to wear. The emphasis here is on handmade furnishings and decorations, be it the tables, chairs, quilts, rugs, curtains, or candle holders, all arranged in the rooms in a restrained manner reminiscent of Shaker dwellings.

Breakfast, served in bed for those who wish, includes imported cheese, sliced fruits, warm Pennsylvania Dutch pastry, and choice of beverage.

Accommodations: 6 rooms, 4 with private toilet and washstand, all with shared shower rooms. *Driving Instructions:* St. Michaels is 9 miles west of Easton on Route 33.

Woodsboro, Maryland

THE ROSEBUD INN

4 North Main Street, Woodsboro, MD 21798. 301-845-2221. *Innkeepers:* Albert and Alice Eaton. Open all year.

So great was Dr. George F. Smith's love for roses and their fragrance that he devoted much of his life to the establishment and operation of the Rosebud Perfume Company in Woodsboro. When in 1920 he decided to construct a residence next to his perfumery, he carried the rose theme throughout the building, especially in the leaded-glass doors of the dining room, which have an elaborate rosebud motif.

Dr. Smith's 2½-story, hip-roofed brick Colonial Revival home is now the Rosebud Inn, purchased in 1980 by Alice and Albert Eaton, who carefully restored most of the building's fifteen rooms. The inn's large porches are supported by fluted Ionic columns topped with terra-cotta scrolls. Within, marble mantels decorate the parlor and living room, and woodwork has been scraped and polished or painted throughout the inn. The hardwood floors on the ground level have interesting geometric-design borders, and the first- and second-floor bay windows are framed by graceful arches.

The inn's guest rooms are large and sunny. In addition to having period bedsteads, each room is provided with an easy chair for lounging and a table and chairs for writing.

Next door to the inn, Dr. Smith's grandchildren still operate the family perfume business.

Accommodations: 5 rooms, 3 with private bath. *Pets:* Not permitted. *Driving Instructions:* Woodsboro is at the junction of Routes 194 and 550 northeast of Frederick.

New Jersey

Cape May, New Jersey

THE ABBEY

Columbia Avenue and Gurney Street, Cape May, NJ 08204. 609-884-4506. *Innkeepers:* Jay and Marianne Schatz. Open April through November.

The Abbey is a Gothic gingerbread fantasy built in 1869 as a summer villa for John B. McCreary, a coal baron and U.S. senator. Because of its architectural significance, it was chosen to be recorded in the Library of Congress. Jay and Marianne Schatz, the two enthusiastic innkeepers, named the place the Abbey and set about restoring it from stem to stern as an inn. The name was chosen to convey the building's resemblance to a Gothic church. Its detailing is highlighted by an authentic, colorful Victorian paint job both inside and out. The Abbey is furnished with an impressive collection of Victorian pieces: ornate tufted velvet chairs and sofas, heavy walnut beds and dressers, Oriental rugs, and even an old harp standing beside a Boston fern in the parlor. The Shatzes have a passion for period lighting fixtures; so it follows that each room has electrified gaslights of every shape, manner, and design. One of the nicest features of the Abbey is its tower room, which affords a panoramic view of the entire town and the Atlantic Ocean. Breakfast is included in the room rate–a Continental breakfast in the summer and a full breakfast in the spring and fall. Visitors who wish to see the Abbey but are unable to stay overnight are invited to tour the first floor at 5 P.M. on Thursdays, Saturdays, and Sundays.

Accommodations: 7 rooms, 4 with private bath. *Pets:* Not permitted. *Driving Instructions:* In Cape May turn left on Ocean Street, go three blocks, and turn left on Columbia Avenue. Drive one block to the inn.

NEW YORK

Lake Hopatcong

Chester

RARITAN BAY

Riegelsville
Milford
Upper Black Eddy
Erwinna
Point Pleasant
Lumberville
Stockton
New Hope
Lambertville
Holicong
Princeton

PENNSYLVANIA

Trenton

Spring Lake

Philadelphia

Delaware River

Raritan River

NEW JERSEY TURNPIKE

GARDEN STATE PARKWAY

ATLANTIC CITY EXPWY

Great Egg Harbor River

Maurice River

DELAWARE BAY

DELAWARE

Cape May

ATLANTIC OCEAN

NEW JERSEY

SCALE OF MILES

BARNARD-GOOD HOUSE

238 Perry Street, Cape May, NJ 08204. 609-884-5381. *Innkeepers: Nan and Tom Hawkins.* Open April through October.

Barnard-Good House is a handsome Second Empire Victorian home complete with dormered mansard roof and wraparound gingerbread-encrusted veranda. Named after the innkeepers' great-grandparents, Barnard-Good House has a first-floor parlor complete with antique pump organ. The room contains a handsome hand-carved and tiled false fireplace. The extravagant piece is typical of the Victorian desire to "keep up with the Joneses" that inspired the building's owners to install this nonworking accessory.

The inn's dining room has a lace-covered dining table over which hangs an authentic iron, pewter, and brass gasolier. The room's sideboard, from 1870, has brass pulls in the shape of griffins. A small Victorian tufted sofa with matching ladies' and gentlemen's chairs resides in the draped bay-window area of the room.

The dining room is where Nan and Tom serve the breakfast that has become the hallmark of Barnard-Good House. During the summer months Nan's breakfast might include freshly squeezed strawberry-orange juice followed by chilled fruit soup, egg and mushroom omelet with avocado garnish, fresh corn casserole, croissants, and lemon pâté-choux with almond-chocolate topping. Other months of the year Nan prepares a somewhat less ambitious Continental breakfast in which her home-baked breads, rolls, and, often, fruit-filled crepes play a central role.

On the second and third floors are the guest rooms and one suite—all named for various members of the innkeepers' families. The Leggatt Room has a striking four-poster canopy bed and matching Victorian dressing table. The color scheme here is blue and gold with toile wallpaper in blue blending with the gold fabric and fringe of the canopy and draped dressing table. The Hawkins Suite has a separate sitting room and full private bath. Perhaps the inn's most flamboyantly Victorian room, it has bold wallpaper displaying enormous birds. Of note is the third-floor bathroom, which has the original copper bathtub (restored by the innkeepers), an antique pull-chain commode, and a marble-topped sink. A stained-glass window completes the Victorian touches.

Outside, the front yard has an unusual bone-shaped concrete-bordered garden that was original to the house and now overflows with yellow and red annual flowers. Hydrangea bushes (Cape May's city flower) surround the veranda and walkway. The picket fence, also original to the house, is adorned with clematis vine.

Accommodations: 6 rooms, 2 with private bath. *Pets:* Not permitted. *Children:* Under twelve not permitted. *Driving Instructions:* Take the Garden State Parkway to the end. Go over the bridge and follow Lafayette Street through two traffic lights. Turn right at the liquor store and drive to the next traffic light.

THE BRASS BED INN

719 Columbia Avenue, Cape May, NJ 08204. 609-884-8075. *Innkeepers:* John and Donna Dunwoody.

The Brass Bed Inn stands just two blocks from the beach in the midst of Cape May's oldest district. The Gothic Revival "cottage" was built in 1872 with separate quarters for the summer kitchen and servants' rooms. The two buildings were joined in 1930, when the establishment first opened as the Woodbine Tourist Home. The Dunwoodys bought the old house in 1980 and began its restoration. In the process they discovered that many of the guest-room furnishings were the originals and still had their 1872 shipping tags on them. This furniture has been restored and remains in the rooms along with the many brass beds that are the special feature that gave this inn its name.

The public rooms are furnished with Dunwoody family heirlooms including a Columbia wind-up Grafonola complete with a collection of early recordings. Ornate plaster crown moldings, ceiling medallions, and 10-foot French doors are typical interior details. Parlor furnishings include a carved rosewood marble-topped table, an Eastlake settee and rocker, and an oaken drop-leaf desk. Guests are served a Continental breakfast in the Victorian dining room, which contains a gasolier. A wide veranda has pretty carpenter's lace gingerbread trim.

Accommodations: 8 rooms, 2 with private bath. *Pets:* Not permitted. *Children:* Under 12 not permitted. *Driving Instructions:* In Cape May take Lafayette Street to Ocean Street, turn left on Ocean, go 3 blocks to Columbia Avenue, turn left, and drive 2½ blocks to the inn, which is on the left.

CAPTAIN MEY'S INN

202 Ocean Street, Cape May, NJ 08204. 609-884-7793 or 884-6793. *Innkeepers:* Carin Feddermann and Milly LaCanfora. Open all year.

This late-Victorian house was built in 1890 by Dr. Walter H. Phillips, a native of Cape May and a noted homeopathic physician. Its inviting interior is filled with Victorian antiques, Tiffany stained glass, and rich oaken woodwork. The particularly handsome dining room has chestnut and oak paneling and a crowned and molded oak ceiling. One wall has a bay window complete with seat and leaded glass. The room's fireplace was recently reopened by the innkeepers, after having been closed for fifty years.

In the Victorian sitting parlor, the innkeepers display their collection of Delft-blue china and Dutch artifacts in a Gothic oaken bookcase. Captain Mey's Dutch ambience extends to its Continental breakfast, at which cheeses such as Gouda and Edam appear along with homebaked breads and hot coffee.

The guest rooms consist of Victorian furnishings — marble-topped dressers, hundred-year-old walnut high-back beds, wicker and upholstered chairs, and lacy curtains. Fresh flowers grace the dressers in the summer. On the beds are handmade quilts, comforters, or brightly colored patchwork crocheted blankets.

Accommodations: 10 rooms, 3 with private bath. *Pets and children under 12:* Not permitted. *Driving Instructions:* The inn is on Ocean Street.

THE CHALFONTE HOTEL

301 Howard Street, Cape May, NJ 08057. 609-884-8409. *Innkeepers*: Anne C. LeDuc and Judy Bartella. Open from Memorial Day through the second week in September.

The Chalfonte Hotel is one of Cape May's architectural gems. It was the only big Victorian hotel to survive the town's disastrous 1878 fire. Built in 1876 by Colonel Henry Sawyer, a Civil War hero who was released from a Confederate prison in exchange for Robert E. Lee's son, the hotel is an enormous Victorian gingerbread affair. It is surrounded by beautiful verandas and balconies framed by gingerbread arches and railings, lots of old rockers, high columns, and green-and-white striped awnings—all contributing to the atmosphere of elegant living in a bygone era. One happy guest described the hotel as a "Victorian lady resplendent in lace trim."

The interior of the Chalfonte is unpretentious and friendly. The old lobby has a lived-in, cozy feeling. It leads into a small library, where there are books of the same vintage as the hotel, and the writing room. The long dining room was, at one time, the ballroom. The guest rooms are large and airy, with no phones or television, and the only air-conditioning is the ocean breeze. The simple turn-of-the-century Victorian furnishings include marble-top bureaus and sinks in the rooms — some even have a washstand with a bowl and pitcher.

Mrs. Calvin Satterfield has owned the hotel since 1915, and the place has been in the Satterfield family since 1907. This lovely lady is from Virginia and brings with her the strong influence of Southern hospitality that prevails here. Mrs. Satterfield, now well on in her eighties, has two enthusiastic managers, Anne LeDuc and Judy Bartella, who undertook restoration of the historic building with two federal matching grants of $10,000, the aid of many friends, students, and supporters, and lots of elbow grease. Work weekends, when architecture students, specialists, and laymen of all ages exchange labor for room and board, take place in the spring and fall. It's not only fun; it's for a good cause. None of this is meant to imply that the old hotel is unprepared to receive her guests. She is ready and most graciously willing.

Dining at the Chalfonte is a real Southern treat. All the meals are cooked by Helen Dickerson, who was asked to help out in the kitchen more than forty years ago and is still here. She and her daughter Dorothy prepare breakfasts of spoon bread, fresh fish, kidney stew, eggs, juice, bacon, and more. Dinners feature daily specials, which might be Southern fried chicken (the real thing), fresh fish, deviled crab, or Virginia ham, and always include fresh New Jersey produce and plenty of Helen's rolls and desserts. Children under eight eat in a separate supervised dining room. A new addition to the hotel is its King Edward Room, a period cocktail bar and lounge. Breakfast and dinner are served to the public also, with reservations.

Accommodations: 102 rooms, a few with private baths. *Pets:* Not permitted. *Driving Instructions:* The hotel is in the heart of Cape May's historic district. Drive to the end of the Garden State Parkway. From the south, cross on the Lewes to Cape May Ferry.

THE GINGERBREAD HOUSE

28 Gurney Street, Cape May, NJ 08204. 609-884-0211. *Innkeepers:* Fred and Joan Echevarria. Open all year.

The Gingerbread House is decorated with elaborate, scrolly Victorian woodwork, which makes it look like a real gingerbread house. It is one of eight identical "cottages," designed by Cape May architect Stephen Decatur Button in the mid-nineteenth century and built in conjunction with the long-gone Stockton Hotel, that were known as the "Stockton Row Cottages." Inside the Gingerbread House, the guests' living room, with its ornate ironwork in the hearth of the working fireplace, is a popular gathering spot for guests. Upstairs is the master bedroom, airy and spacious in keeping with the age of the house. Here guests have their own private porch where the roar of the ocean can be heard and the sea can be glimpsed over the boardwalk just one block away. This is a warm, friendly place whose Victorian soul has been considerably enlivened by Fred and Joan's use of clear, fresh colors and a tasteful amount of period furnishings.

Accommodations: 6 rooms, 1 with private bath. *Pets:* Not permitted. *Children:* Under six not permitted. *Driving Instructions:* Take Route 109 (Lafayette Street) to the first light (Madison Avenue) and turn left. Go 3 blocks to Columbia Avenue and turn right; then turn left at Gurney Street.

THE MAINSTAY INN

635 Columbia Avenue, Cape May, NJ 08204. 609-884-8690. *Innkeepers:* Tom and Sue Carroll. Open April through October.

If you should want to return to an era gone by, it is hard to imagine a place more happily restored and appropriate than the Mainstay, originally the creation of architect S. D. Button who was commissioned on a "spare no expense basis" to design a clubhouse for two wealthy gamblers. The result was an 1872 villa where the two owners entertained their friends in a luxurious setting—fourteen-foot ceilings, ornate plaster moldings, elaborate chandeliers, sweeping veranda, and a fine cupola. Tom and Sue Carroll have retained the lovely atmosphere of this house in their bed-and-breakfast inn. Great care has been taken to decorate each room with fine Victorian antiques and attractive quilted bed covers. Most of the bedrooms are large, with ornate headboards, marble-topped dressers, 10-foot mirrors, and elaborate armoires. Five spacious rooms are available in the nearby Mainstay Cottage, built in 1870. The cupola offers a grand view of the town and ocean. On the veranda are two porch swings large enough for two people to stretch out in and take in the soothing Victorian atmosphere. For visitors to Cape May who are unable to stay at the inn itself, the Carrolls are happy to provide tours of the ground floor at 4:00 P.M. on Tuesdays, Thursdays, Saturdays, and Sundays, with afternoon tea following each tour. Breakfast for house guests is included in the room rate and is likely to be quite special. In addition to the more usual offerings at this meal, the Carrolls sometimes serve special dishes such as strawberry crepes or quiche Lorraine.

Accommodations: 11 rooms, 7 with private bath. *Pets and Children:* Not permitted. *Driving Instructions:* Take the Garden State Parkway to the end. It becomes Lafayette Street. Turn left at the first light (Madison Avenue), and then turn right on Columbia Avenue. The inn is three blocks up on the right.

POOR RICHARD'S INN

17 Jackson Street, Cape May, NJ 08204. 609-884-3536. *Innkeepers*: Richard and Harriett Samuelson. Open April through October.

Poor Richard's Inn was built in 1882 by George Hildreth, who, at the time, owned the Wyoming Hotel next door (now called the Carroll Villa). The building remained a private home until the early 1970s. Individually listed in the National Register of Historic Places, it has recently had the finishing touches of restoration work completed by its current owners. This final restoration has included the installation of a new slate roof, as well as the use of five earth-tone colors of paint to accent the gingerbread detail. The use of these colors distinguishes many of Cape May's finest restorations.

The inn lacks public rooms but has spacious bedrooms and breezy porches. For this reason it would be appropriate to consider Poor Richard's a guest house rather than an inn. The rooms are filled with original artwork by the innkeepers, expatriate New York artists, and many oak pieces from the turn of the century, as well as quilts,

baskets, rockers, and pine furniture from the same period.

Accommodations: 9 rooms, 3 with private bath. *Children:* Welcome if "well behaved." *Driving Instructions:* Take the Garden State Parkway to the end. Follow signs into town straight through until you reach a fork in the road. Take the left fork (Jackson Street) one block.

THE QUEEN VICTORIA

102 Ocean Street, Cape May, NJ 08204. 609-884-8702. *Innkeepers:* Dane and Joan Wells. Open all year.

The Queen Victoria was built in 1881 as a summer home. A century later it was restored to its former Victorian appearance by innkeepers Dane and Joan Wells. Joan, a former director of the Victorian Society, is a Victoriana buff. The bookshelves here are well stocked with works on local history, Victorian antiques, and architecture. Fires are lighted in the parlor's brick hearth on cold days. The parlor is furnished in Mission antiques, and the guest rooms contain period wicker, walnut, and pine pieces. There are several brass beds and even one old-fashioned four-poster. Handmade quilts adorn each bed, and fresh flowers are placed in each room, no matter what the season. The Wellses provide nice little extras for their guests: Beds are turned down at night, a piece of home-made fudge is placed on each pillow, and fluffy robes are provided for guests whose rooms share baths, although every room has an old-fashioned sink.

A buffet breakfast each morning features freshly squeezed juices, nut and fruit breads, and perhaps an egg casserole or homemade granola. Afternoon tea is accompanied by finger sandwiches or "fresh from the oven" cookies. During the day, a favorite pastime is taking one of the inn's bicycles out for a tour of the town; there is even a bicycle built for two.

Accommodations: 13 rooms, 5 with private bath. *Pets:* Not permitted. *Driving Instructions:* In Cape May, take Lafayette Street to Ocean Street (second light). Turn left, and drive 3 blocks to the inn.

THE 7TH SISTER GUESTHOUSE

10 Jackson Street, Cape May, NJ 08204. 609-884-2280. *Innkeepers*: Bob and Jo-Anne Echevarria Myers. Open all year.

The 7th Sister Guesthouse, built in 1888, is one of seven identical Victorian-Renaissance Revival houses designed by the noted Philadelphia architect Stephen Decatur Button. Local legend holds that each house was built for one of seven maiden daughters of a wealthy Victorian baron, but the story appears to be apocryphal. The seven houses front on an interior courtyard known as Atlantic Terrace; five houses have their backs to Jackson Street. Because the houses predated a formal street-numbering system, the gas company that supplied gas for the original gas lamps assigned street numbers to each house for billing purposes. Thus the Guesthouse received its bills as No. 7, the seventh sister. It still gets its bills that way today, although official records now list the house as No. 10.

The 7th Sister, listed on the National Register of Historic Places, retains about 80 percent of its original furniture, augmented by a collection of more than fifty wicker pieces. A magnificent central circular staircase leads the guests to seven ocean-view guest rooms, which are furnished with Victorian bureaus, washstands, plants, and original paintings by Jo-Anne. A guest living room overlooks the ocean and has a fire in the fireplace during the winter months. Now and again, the old player piano can be heard above the roar of the ocean. No meals are served.

Accommodations: 6 rooms with shared baths. *Pets:* Not permitted. *Children:* Under eight not permitted. *Driving Instructions:* Take the Garden State Parkway to the end, where it becomes Route 109 and finally Lafayette Street. Take Lafayette to the end (Jackson Street), turn left, and the guest house is the last on the right.

WINDWARD HOUSE

24 Jackson Street, Cape May, NJ 08204. 609-884-3368. *Inn-keepers:* Owen and Sandy Miller. Open March through November.

Windward House, a typical seashore shingle cottage of the 1900s, is handsome when viewed from the street, but its interior makes it special. Windward House was built in 1905 by a wealthy doctor who also built an adjacent cottage on the property for his mistress. The cottage is a smaller version of the main house. In a moment of divided loyalty to wife and mistress the doctor had the banister casings in the staircases of both houses fitted with hand-carved hearts. Windward House is a fine restoration showing the skills not only of the present owners, but of Tom and Sue Carroll who did much of the work before they moved on to their present inn, the Mainstay (also in Cape May). Throughout Windward House is a selection of period pieces that form a sampler of the colonial through late Victorian eras. These pieces are set off by polished hardwood floors, Oriental and other carpeting, and several doors with beveled glass (in one case) or stained-glass lights.

Windward House was one of the first in town to be built with a large central hall, opening onto which are the spacious living room, parlor, and dining room. Time and time again one's attention is drawn to the windows, in part because there are sixty-four throughout the building. Glass of many colors forms scenes — some of a nautical theme — and patterns of colored light.

Each guest room is decorated in a different style from the Victorian period and features furniture described as Renaissance, Eastlake, Jenny Lind spool, Empire, and so forth. Windward House has three large porches for lounging and sunning. Access to two porches is from guest rooms through French doors that have stained-glass transoms. Rooms at Windward are properly Victorian in their large size. The Empire Room, for example, has both an antique double bed and a single bed; the Chippendale Room has a pair of three-quarter Chippendale beds with a matching highboy and lowboy. The Cottage Room has a pair of double brass beds and curved glass windows overlooking historic Jackson Street. For guests who prefer not to walk upstairs, the Renaissance Room has its own small sitting area and an antique double bed as well as a private bath. In addition to rooms available on a nightly basis, Windward House offers a spacious two-bedroom English apartment that can accommodate five and has its own kitchen, bathroom, private entrance, and off-street parking. The apartment is rented on a weekly-or-longer basis. Other than a Continental breakfast no meals are served at Windward House.

Accommodations: 7 rooms, 5 with private bath. *Pets:* Not permitted. *Driving Instructions:* Take the Garden State Parkway to the southern end; continue into Cape May on Lafayette Street to Jackson Street (dead-end), then turn left and drive through the Mall to 24 Jackson Street.

Chester, New Jersey

PUBLICK HOUSE

111 Main Street, Chester, NJ 07930. 201-879-6878. *Innkeeper:*
John Dering. Open all year except New Year's Day.

The Publick House began life as a tavern in 1810, the creation of
Zephaniah Drake. The three-story brick building was considered the
most elegant hostelry of its day. Stagecoaches stopped here on their
travels between Jersey City—known then as Paulus Hook—and
Easton, Pennsylvania. In the mid-nineteenth century the inn was run
as the Chester Institute, a college preparatory school. Its founder,
Mr. William Rankin, added the two three-story wings that may have
spelled the end of the Institute, for in 1862 the place was sold and once
again became a hotel. It had been the Brick Hotel and was now called
Chester Inn, a name it carried for most of its innkeeping life. The inn
today is on both the New Jersey and national registers of historic
places. Plans for the building are in the records of the Library of
Congress. The architecture of the Publick House lies somewhere

between Victorian and Federal. Every room, including the second- and third-floor guest rooms, has its own fireplace with carved mantel and brick hearth. The staircase and mantelpieces are still intact, as are the chandeliers and tin ceilings.

The Black River and Raritan Publick House, as it is officially known, has undergone years of restoration by the present owners, Jeff Beers and Jack Welsh of Growth Enterprises, Inc. They bought the inn in 1976 and promptly commissioned architect Alexander A. Bol of Union, New Jersey to turn back time and restore the old inn to its former lines. Layers of paint were blasted off the Flemish bond brick, and sealers were put on for preservation. The front porch was replaced by a two-story porch carefully duplicated from the nineteenth-century original. Pictures and plans of the hotel were supplied by the Chester Historical Society from the originals done by the WPA in the 1930s.

Each of the inn's dining rooms, which are its mainstay, has been carefully redone around a particular theme, such as The Larder, The Parlor, and The Tack Room. Menus offer an array of traditional hotel fare. The Barber Shop Lounge has drinks and entertainment almost every evening.

The guest rooms, on the second and third floors, are furnished with antiques spanning several centuries. There are old rockers, gilded frame mirrors of simple lines, at least one green plant per room, and braided scatter rugs on the dark wood floors. The rooms are austere in an attractive way reminiscent of earlier times. The walls are covered with old-fashioned small-figure print wallpapers, and some of the beds have heavy antique spreads. Some of the rooms feature small sitting rooms just off the bedroom; others offer traditional lodgings with antique double beds.

Accommodations: 9 rooms with private bath. *Driving Instructions:* From Morristown, New Jersey, take Route 24 west. The Main Street of Chester is Route 24.

Lambertville, New Jersey

Lambertville is on the Delaware River about 17 miles north of Trenton and a short drive from *Washington Crossing Park* to the south, site of the landing of Washington and his troops on their historic march on Trenton. There is skiing at *Belle Mountain,* about 5 miles to the south on Route 29, and boating on the Delaware River in the summer. The area abounds with flea markets, some open all year. Visitors who wish to tour historic Bucks County, Pennsylvania, may cross at Lambertville to the New Hope side of the river or farther south at Washington Crossing to see the Pennsylvania park and museum.

LAMBERTVILLE HOUSE

32 Bridge Street, Lambertville, NJ 08530. 609-397-0202. *Innkeeper*: Susan Darrah. Open all year except Christmas.

Lambertville House was first opened for travelers in 1812 by Senator John Lambert when the small hotel served as a stagecoach stop in the village, then called Coryell's Ferry. Over the years the hotel has been host to a number of illustrious guests, including Baron Renfrew, later to become King Edward VII; Andrew Johnson; Ulysses S. Grant; Tom Thumb; and Pearl White, star of *Perils of Pauline,* the early movie serial melodrama.

Located in the center of the town of Lambertville, the hotel is distinguished by a two-story gingerbread porch, which projects out from a simple four-story façade. Inside the hotel is comfortable and old-fashioned, with the look of the nineteenth century fairly well preserved in the rooms. Some public rooms have the acoustic ceiling tiles of larger inns and hotels, and the common-room furnishings are not all antiques, but there are a number of nice pieces around, and the wallpapers, exposed brick walls, and small-paned windows contribute to the ambience.

The Lambert Room has a broad fireplace surmounted by a mantel that flows easily into the chair-height paneled wainscoting around the room. A fine old print hangs over the fireplace, and a built-in cupboard contains a small display of antique china. The Buttery is an English-style pub with vaulted ceiling and exposed brick walls where food is served, as well as in the Lambert Room and the 1812 Room.

The menu at the inn draws heavily on American cooking. Appetizers include several seafood offerings and stuffed mushrooms. There are several soups, all homemade, followed by a choice of about 12 entrées such as roast duckling, stuffed chicken breast, tenderloin tips garnished with mushrooms, and roast prime ribs of beef.

Accommodations: 31 rooms, 5 with private bath. *Pets:* Not permitted. *Driving Instructions:* The inn may be reached by taking Route 29 north from Trenton or Route 202 south from Flemington.

CHESTNUT HILL

63 Church Street, Milford, NJ 08848. 201-995-9761. *Innkeepers:* Linda and Rob Castagna. Open all year.

The real-estate agent's car hadn't even stopped when Rob and Linda Castagna declared this to be exactly what they wanted. The Victorian house is near a bank of the Delaware River, separated from it only by seldom-used railroad tracks. The yard is shaded by an immense beech tree. Built in the 1860s, the house spent its first hundred years under the ownership of two wealthy families whose servants and handymen kept its paint and parquet floors like new. Rob and Linda were thus able to have the fun of decorating without the agony of a major renovation. Walls throughout were papered with an array of floral prints, each creating a special mood. Pineapple Room is spacious and sunny and has a spool bed topped with a Scottish comforter. Another room, in soft grayish blues, has antique furnishings, a puffy quilt, and old-fashioned shutters at the windows. The second-floor hall bathroom is a tiled fantasy with all original fixtures, pretty papers, and a crystal chandelier. Guests enjoy a full country breakfast in the formal dining room with its plant-filled bay window. The parlor and halls are decorated with early pictures of the house. The floor-to-ceiling windows in the parlor afford excellent views of the river.

Accommodations: 3 rooms with shared bath. *Pets:* Not permitted. *Smoking:* Discouraged. *Driving Instructions:* Take Route 519 to Milford. Church Street is just one block from the bridge. The road curves to the left, and the house is the last on the left.

PEACOCK INN

20 Bayard Lane (Route 206), Princeton, NJ 08540. 609-924-1707. *Innkeepers*: Mr. and Mrs. Francis C. Swain. Open all year.

The Peacock Inn is an attractive Colonial building now located just off Nassau Street, the main street of this lovely little town. The inn was on the tax roll in 1775 but was moved from the campus of Princeton one hundred years later. Originally a private home, Peacock Inn has been taking in travelers since 1912. Its address, one block from the Princeton campus, is partly responsible for the inn's roster of illustrious guests, such as Bertrand Russell, Albert Einstein, and F. Scott Fitzgerald, who have come from all over the world to this gambrel-roofed inn with high dormers, multipaned windows, and big front porch.

The inn, primarily a restaurant, offers guest rooms on the second and third floors. Nine have private baths, and all are comfortable—as the Swains point out, "old fashioned, but genteel." While there are eleven fireplaces throughout the old house, insurance costs prevent their use. The inn is quite popular on university weekends, so reservations are a must.

The dining areas and bar on the main floor are pleasant colonial-style rooms that serve approximately twelve entrées from a blackboard menu. Three-quarters of the varied American cuisine is fresh seafood. The specialties are sautéed scallops, flounder stuffed with broccoli, and Southern fried chicken. No breakfast is served, but the dining rooms are open to both guests and the public for lunch and dinner.

Accommodations: 15 rooms, 9 with private bath. *Pets:* allowed occasionally; be sure to ask. *Driving Instructions:* Princeton is on Route 27, just off Route 1. The inn is one block from the campus on Bayard Lane, just off Nassau Street.

Spring Lake, New Jersey

ASHLING COTTAGE

106 Sussex Avenue, Spring Lake, NJ 07762. 201-449-3553. *Innkeeper:* Howard Falk. Open daily late May through mid-September; weekends only in April and early and mid-May, and from mid-September through January 1.

Ashling cottage was built in 1877 by carpenter George Hulett, who lived there with his wife, Hannah, until 1892. Hulett seems to have loved diversity, for every room is unique, with such features as step-up and step-down bath, dormer windows, individual porches, and wainscoting-enclosed closets. The owners of Ashling Cottage, Howard and Sheila Falk, spent a decade visiting inns in the United States and Canada before putting their ideas into practice at Spring Lake. Each guest room contains antique pieces brought back to New Jersey from their many trips. In decorating the cottage for its present use, they chose fabrics, wallpapers, and furnishings that emphasize the special features Hulett put into the home more than a century ago.

Each guest room contains a queen-sized bed and has carefully coordinated drapes, curtains, quilts, and linens. Breakfast, served in a glass-enclosed solarium resplendent with palms and white wicker chairs and tables, typically consists of home-baked breads and freshly squeezed juice and freshly ground coffee.

The parlor and living room, like the rest of the house, are furnished with oaken antiques including a rolltop desk, tables, oak and leather rockers, and upholstered couches. Across from the cottage is a large spring-fed lake spanned by picturesque wooden bridges and surrounded by beautifully maintained park grounds.

Accommodations: 11 rooms, 9 with private bath. *Pets:* Not permitted. *Driving Instructions:* Take Garden State Parkway to exit 98, then Route 34 south 1.5 miles to Allaire Road, then east to Spring Lake.

THE NORMANDY INN

21 Tuttle Avenue, Spring Lake, NJ 07762. 201-449-7172. *Innkeepers:* Frank and Marcia O'Keefe. Open May 15 to October 15.

The Normandy Inn is an old-fashioned Victorian seaside inn. Built in 1888 and less than a block from the ocean and New Jersey's famous sandy beaches, it is all turrets, gables, shutters, and porches. A very large porch that wraps around the house has been partially enclosed. The surrounding neighborhood is filled with many homes of the same vintage. The lobby–sitting area of the Normandy is furnished with Victorian antiques and Oriental rugs, and a fire is often set in the fireplace on cool evenings.

The guest rooms retain the atmosphere of the late nineteenth-century. Each room has something a little different or special to set it apart. One has its own small private porch overlooking the sea. A favorite, the circular tower room, is particularly appealing. Several rooms look out to the ocean, and a second-floor veranda is available for guests' use. The inn's dining room is open to guests and their friends for big Irish breakfasts.

Spring Lake, known as New Jersey's "Irish Riviera," is noted for its peaceful (that is, noncommercial) boardwalk. The area abounds with marinas, lakes, and rolling horse pastures. Golf, tennis, and historic sites are nearby. Many boutiques in town feature Irish goods.

Accommodations: 22 rooms, 18 with private bath and 4 sharing hall baths. *Driving Instructions:* Take exit 98 off the Garden State Parkway to Route 34. Follow the signs east on Route 524 to Spring Lake.

Stockton, New Jersey

THE WOOLVERTON INN

Woolverton Road, Stockton, New Jersey. Mailing address: Box
233-A, R.D. 3, Stockton, NJ 08559. 609-397-0802.

A recent addition to the growing number of country inns in the Bucks
County–Hunterdon County region is the Woolverton Inn in Stockton. Operating as bed-and-breakfast inn only since the fall of 1981,
the Woolverton Inn is a blend of two distinctly different architectures.
The stone manor house was built in 1793 by John Prall, a local
entrepreneur who ran a quarry, the remains of which can be seen at
the end of the inn gardens. Prall also ran the gristmill nearby, at the
confluence of Wichecheoke Creek and the Delaware River. The river
was an important artery of commerce in the early nineteenth century,
and the prosperity of John Prall can easily be measured by the quality
of the house he built. In the latter half of the century the manor was
remodeled by Maurice Woolverton, whose major contribution was an
Italianate mansard roof.

The entire front of the Woolverton is galleried; the upstairs porch
is bordered by handsome pierced-wood balusters and railing. Flag-

stone patios descend to the manicured formal gardens planted by Whitney North Seymour, who owned the Woolverton Inn from 1939 to 1957. The property was then purchased by St. John Terrell, the owner of the popular Music Circus. During these years, many celebrities who were performing at the Circus were entertained at the inn.

Because the Woolverton Inn has resisted the temptation to add a restaurant to its public rooms, the parlor, kitchen, and dining rooms remain exclusively for houseguests' use. Each of these rooms is antique-filled: period upholstered furniture and Oriental rugs in the living room, more formal mahogany chairs and table set before a paneled mantelpiece in one dining room. The country kitchen has wide pine floors, ladder-back rush-seat chairs, and barn-red built-in cabinets.

A variety of beds are used in the Woolverton Inn's guest rooms. In one, a graceful arch-topped, canopied bed has matching dust ruffle and canopy cover. In another, a pair of twin four-posters, whose posts rise as high as a man, are set off by the wide-board pine floor, a time-softened russet Oriental rug, and an Empire rocker. Most rooms have six- or nine-panel doors with turn-of-the-century iron and ceramic hardware. The doors, like most of the trim in the inn, are painted white or teal blue.

Accommodations: 9 rooms with shared baths. *Pets:* Not permitted. *Driving Instructions:* Take Route 29 north into Stockton. Take Route 523 for ⅛ mile and turn left on Woolverton Road. The inn is at the second drive on the right.

New York

Alexandria Bay, New York

THOUSAND ISLANDS CLUB-RESORT
   Country Road, Wellesley Island, Alexandria Bay, NY 13607.
   315-482-2551. *Innkeeper:* Kenneth Stebles. Open Memorial Day
   through Columbus Day.

The Thousand Islands Club, which occupies the eastern portion of
Wellesley Island near Alexandria Bay, was initially developed in the
first part of this century by George C. Boldt, whose extensive farm
holdings in the area provided some of the produce consumed at his
Waldorf-Astoria and Bellevue-Stratford hotels. Boldt also built the
unfinished 300-room castle on nearby Boldt's Island, which remains
today one of the area's most popular tourist stops. In its earlier days,
the Thousand Islands Club was a highly exclusive millionaire's
paradise, but it has mellowed over the years and now accepts guests.
The club occupies more than a thousand acres on the island and has
full resort facilities, including an 18-hole USGA golf course, tennis
courts, and heated swimming pools. Horseback riding is nearby, and
boat tours can be arranged.

   The main clubhouse is a two- and three-story Mediterranean-style
hotel with arched windows, Mediterranean-style roofs, and a
swimming pool at the door. Built in 1910, the clubhouse contains
twenty-eight guest rooms and the main lobby and dining room, as well
as a gift shop, bar, and golf shop. In addition, there are numerous
cottages, a small motel unit called Pergola, and a stuccoed Swiss
Chalet with its many-gabled roof. The Chalet offers sixteen
additional guest rooms.

   The resort is directly on the St. Lawrence River-Seaway, and river
activities are very much part of a stay here. River life at the resort
centers on the covered walkway and boat-slip area that leads from

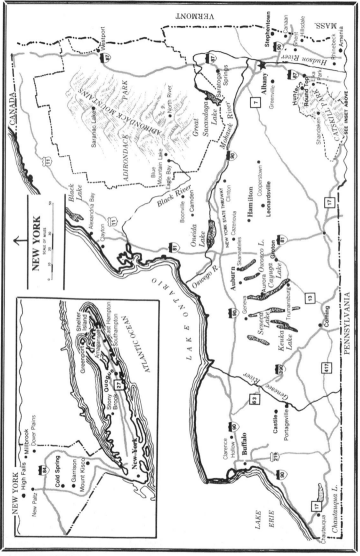

shore to the Quarter Deck, an enclosed meeting room at the end of the dock. Youngsters may fish from the long dock, but serious fishermen hire boats and, often, local guides to spend a day on the river challenging the plentiful supply of black bass, pike, and muskellunge. The resort's staff will be happy to prepare fish caught by guests.

The Thousand Islands Club serves meals to all guests. The menu includes a wider number of selections than many, and the quality of food preparation is high. Dinners start with a choice of appetizers such as clams casino, escargots, or seafood au gratin. This is followed by a choice of two or three daily soups, almost always available is the house specialty, baked French-Canadian onion soup, and usually a cream soup or consommé is an alternative. The Thousand Islands Club has a large salad bar featuring its original-recipe Thousand Island dressing—from the same recipe an inspired chef created for Mr. Boldt more than fifty years ago. In addition to the usual salad selections, the salad bar offers several homemade chutneys and other relishes. There are generally seven or eight entrées each night. Typical selections might include roast beef, duckling à l'orange, frogs' legs, veal scallopine, New York–sirloin steaks, and scallops. The menu changes daily and reflects the seasonal market.

Accommodations: 44 rooms with private bath, plus cottages and motel unit. *Driving Instructions:* Take I-81 across the 1000 Islands Bridge to Exit 51, on Wellesley Island. Turn right on Island Highway and then left on Country Road.

Amagansett, New York

THE MILL GARTH

Windmill Lane, Amagansett, NY 11930. 516-267-3757. *Innkeepers:* Wendy and Burton Van Deusen. Open all year.

Here is one of those romantic places you have always been looking for. Mill Garth is a collection of idyllic garden cottages and small apartments, each decorated and furnished with exquisite taste. It is situated on a quiet little country road, a half mile from the ocean and just on the outskirts of the village of Amagansett. This peaceful and lovely property is centered on a converted farmhouse surrounded by spacious lawns and fields divided by hedges and statuary. There are private patios shaded by towering trees and ivy-clad fences outside many of the cottages.

The Mill Garth sits on the site of one of Long Island's largest windmills. Built in 1797, it burned some years later, but a smaller facsimile of the original is still on the property. In 1881, Sam Babcock built the Windmill Cottage (the main house) for Abraham and Ellen Parsons and their seven children. Mr. Parsons was the miller at the old windmill until his death in 1896. Mrs. Parsons took in boarders at the turn of the century, and the inn's popularity grew. The inn today is quite popular with theater, advertising, and movie people who like to stay here during filmings or while performing at the John Drew Theater at Guild Hall in East Hampton.

The entire Mill Garth complex comprises the main farmhouse and five cottages, all converted from the farm's outbuildings. There is the Gazebo, with its octagonal living room and ceiling woodwork exposed to reveal the roof's handsome underpinnings. The Dairy House has a wood-paneled living room complete with skylight and working fireplace. This ivy-covered cottage was once simply a tiny storage shed and is now a jewel of a studio apartment. And then — the Carriage House, the pièce de resistance, sporting a 22-foot living room with exposed beams, a brick fireplace, and a completely private patio.

The main house contains three suites downstairs and four upstairs. Each has its own private entrance, each is as carefully decorated as someone's own home. There are fully equipped kitchens, comfortable living rooms and separate bedrooms, private telephones, an unusual assortment of original art, and a collection of antiques of all periods that blend with the inn's modern and traditional pieces.

Something of a local secret till now, the Mill Garth does no advertising. It doesn't need any. The summer months are almost always fully rented a year in advance. It is in the off season that the Mill Garth begins to function as a more traditional inn, with overnight or weekend guests vying for reservations. At any time of year it pays to make reservations early.

Accommodations: 13 rooms with private bath. *Pets:* Not permitted. *Driving Instructions:* Windmill Lane runs north off the Montauk Highway (Route 27) just as you enter the western end of Amagansett village.

TROUTBECK

Leedsville Road, Amenia, NY 12501. 914-373-8581. *Innkeepers:* James Flaherty and Robert Skibsted. Open all year — weekdays as an executive conference center and weekends to the public as an inn.

A row of 200-foot sycamores guard the entrance to Troutbeck, a lush baronial retreat. The building is a large Tudor manor house secluded amid more than 400 acres of parklike grounds and forests. This is not an ordinary inn; it falls somewhere between an executive conference center, which it is on weekdays, and a superb private home for a small number of paying guests on weekends.

The entire house and a nearby eighteenth-century farmhouse annex are lavishly decorated. Throughout the main house one finds dark woods, Oriental carpets, wood stoves, and comfortable chintz-covered sofas and chairs. The decor is an appealing blend of heirloom antiques, art objects, and discreet reproductions.

The stone-and-slate English-style estate house was constructed in 1917 by Joel and Amy Spingarn. Joel Spingarn, a horticulturist and literary critic, helped W. E. B. DuBois and Booker T. Washington resolve their differences, and together they founded the NAACP here at Troutbeck. The main house has leaded glass windows, walled formal gardens out on the hill nearby, and many working fireplaces, two in bedrooms. The house, although it contains 28 rooms, is actually rather intimate, with just 12 guest rooms. There are more guest rooms across a curved stone bridge in the Century, Troutbeck's eighteenth-century American farmhouse. All guest rooms feature canopy or four-poster beds.

Guests have the run of the estate, with its hundreds of acres for hiking and tennis, a solar-heated swimming pool, and well-stocked liquor cabinets in both the main house and the farmhouse. The innkeepers take great pride in the food at Troutbeck. The meals have received much acclaim from newspapers and magazines. Specialties are a thick prime rib of beef with Yorkshire pudding, poached salmon with dill hollandaise (in season), and pork tenderloin à l'orange.

Accommodations: 25 rooms with private bath. *Pets:* Not permitted. *Children:* Under one or over twelve permitted. *Driving Instructions:* Given by the inn when reservations are made.

Auburn, New York

Auburn is at the head of Owasco Lake in the Finger Lakes region of New York State. There are many old homes throughout its neighborhoods. Open to the public is the *Home of Harriet Tubman*, who began the Underground Railroad as a means of escape for Southern slaves. The *Cayuga Museum of History and Art* at 203 Genesee Street features exhibits and films pertaining to the history of talking pictures. *Hoopes Memorial Park*, on Route 20 at East Genesee Street, contains a little lake and surrounding rose gardens. In summer, band concerts are held here. Emerson Park at the south end of the lake contains a reproduction of an *Owasco Stockaded Indian Village*. There is a museum here and swimming and picnicking facilities.

SPRINGSIDE INN

41 West Lake Road, Auburn, NY 13021. 315-252-7247. *Innkeepers:* Bill and Barbara Dove. Open February through December.

The Springside Inn is a chef-owned hostelry (to be true to innkeeping tradition, that is how it should be). The rambling Victorian building constructed in 1850 as a private boys' school is on 8 landscaped acres of lawns and trees across the road from Owasco Lake in the heart of the Finger Lakes region of New York State. A wide lawn in front of the inn is shaded by weeping willows and evergreens. A spring-fed pond is the home of a family of ducks. The red clapboard inn has several long, low additions fanning out off either side with striped canvas awnings shading their verandas. Drinks and light snacks are served on the terrace in summer. Its long white balustrade forms an orderly backdrop for the profusion of flowers and shrubs growing in front and hanging in baskets. Flowers are everywhere at the Springside: in tubs, baskets, gardens, and window boxes. Inside the inn each season is celebrated with appropriate flowers and decorations.

Springside Inn features a popular restaurant with a fairly extensive menu of steaks and seafood dishes. House specialties include prime ribs of beef, lobster Newburg, duckling, soufflés, and a fisherman's platter with crab, scallops, scrod, and lobster. Chef Bill Dove whips up a "very special occasion dinner" for two, with duckling and prime ribs, champagne or wine, and a flaming dessert. Dinners and brunches in Autumn and on Sunday incorporate local arts and crafts shows. In July and August a Summer Dinner Theater at the inn attracts visitors from far and wide. The theater, with performances by a professional company, is now in its second decade.

The hotel is proud of its large collection of antique lighting fixtures. The dining rooms are lit by the many attractive and unusual hanging oil lamps suspended from the crisscross of exposed beams and rafters. The antiques used throughout the inn blend with the traditional hotel décor. The guest rooms are immaculate and welcoming with antiques and floral prints. A basket filled with a complimentary Continental breakfast is provided for each guest.

Owasco Lake provides recreational and sightseeing opportunities. There are weekend sailboat races, and excellent fishing, swimming, and boating can be found just minutes from the Springside. In winter cross-country skiing can be enjoyed right behind the inn, and there is ice skating on the lake and ponds.

Accommodations: 8 rooms, 3 with private bath. *Pets:* Not permitted. *Driving Instructions:* Take exit 40 on the New York Thruway to Route 34 south and then Route 38 south to Auburn. The inn is on Route 38 south on Owasco Lake, just 3 minutes from downtown Auburn.

Aurora, New York

It was in Aurora that Henry Wells conceived the idea of the Wells Fargo Stagecoach Line, and here that he founded *Wells College* in 1868. Early visitors to the inn described below were advised to take the stagecoach from Auburn, at a fare of six shillings. Although stagecoach service is a thing of the past, Wells College seniors still ride to graduation in a genuine Wells Fargo stagecoach. Aurora has recently been designated a national historic landmark.

AURORA INN

Main Street (Route 90), Aurora, NY 13026. 315-364-8842. *Innkeepers:* William Eberhardt and Linda Harnett. Open April through Thanksgiving.

Unlike Cornell University, which is "Far above Cayuga's Waters," the Aurora Inn is at its very edge. The inn began its life as a stagecoach stop in 1833, and its reputation as a comfortable place to stay was quickly established. Recently the paint was sandblasted off the old brick, which now reveals its mellow, century-and-a-half-old color. Guests enter the inn through a pillared entryway to the main lobby, where extensive recent renovation has stripped the old floors, painted the moldings around a historical mural a rich cream color, and added Oriental carpeting and brass chandeliers. Two parlors off the central lobby are done in floral prints and furnished with overstuffed chairs and sofas. There is a small dining room used for special college and other private dinners, a somewhat casual bar where college students frequently congregate, and the more formal dining room with its Queen Anne–style furniture and its impressive wall of picture windows affording views of the lake.

The à la carte menu at the inn offers such starters as stuffed mushroom caps, artichokes vinaigrette, shrimp cocktail, and two daily soups. The entrées, numbering about a dozen, include chicken Kiev, London broil, baked ham and turkey with Mornay sauce, fillet of lemon sole, and veal scallopine. A special Sunday menu includes some of these offerings but leans more to roasts of lamb, beef, or pork. In the warmer months drinks are served on the terrace overlooking the lake.

Each guest room is decorated in a slightly different way, although all are covered with "country-style" print wallpapers and have conventional comfortable furniture. Some have a view of the lake, and half of the rooms have private baths.

The inn is owned by Wells College; one of the advantages of a stay here is that guests are invited to use the college's extensive recreational facilities, which include indoor and outdoor swimming, tennis, golf, sailing, and bicycling.

Accommodations: 16 rooms, 8 with private bath. *Pets:* Permitted only with advance notification. *Driving Instructions:* Take exit 40 from the New York Thruway. Follow Route 34 south to Auburn. Take NYS Arterial (old Route 5 and 20) west to Route 90 and go south on it to Aurora.

Blue Mountain Lake, New York

THE HEDGES ON BLUE MOUNTAIN LAKE

Blue Mountain Lake, NY 12812. 518-352-7325. *Innkeepers:* Richard J. and Catherine S. Van Yperen. Open June 18 to Columbus Day.

The Hedges is a complex of two lodges dating from 1880 to 1922 plus fourteen cottages of recent construction. The Hedges is nestled on 12 acres of landscaped lakefront property on the azure lake of its name. All the rooms here have unique decor and include antique furnishings. There are two large lounging rooms with fireplaces, a game room in a log cabin, a large library, and a spacious dining room in a separate building. The dining room is noted for its original watercolor and oil paintings of the Adirondacks. Two of the guest rooms have fireplaces. No room is more than 100 feet from the dock. Recreational facilities include tennis on the Hedges clay court, boating (rentals at the town livery), fishing, swimming, and canoeing.

The Hedges property was originally developed by Hiram B.

Duryea, a Brigadier General in the U.S. Reserves who had served in the Civil War. Duryea's son had discovered numerous new uses for corn starch, and his father had parlayed the ideas into a multimillion-dollar starch empire. In 1880 the senior Duryea purchased the land in the Adirondacks and began construction of the lodges. Duryea drove his workmen hard, insisting that no stone or massive beam be placed in position without his personal supervision. One worker, sick of Duryea's meticulous demands, cut a stone and put it in place without approval. The General discovered the errant stone and made the mason remove it and begin over with a new stone cut in its place. The mason cut the new stone and then dramatically threw it into the lake. Duryea fired him on the spot. Apparently the General's demanding nature wore down even the most loyal of his family members. One evening in 1914, while the business tycoon slept in his Brooklyn mansion, his son Chester crept into his room and shot him. He later told police that angels had commanded him to do it.

In time the estate with its main lodges was bought by the caretaker for the Vanderbilts' large summer estate in the area. The property was converted to a hotel and operated as a rustic establishment without plumbing or electricity for a number of years. Since that time, it has been fully developed and modernized in keeping with a charming, rustic family resort. The lodge continues to receive acclaim in national magazines as one of the best family vacation resorts in the country. Thanks to its small size and personal management by the Van Yperens, it continues to be a small resort with a country inn feeling.

Two meals are served daily in the Hedges dining room. One entrée is served nightly, along with a salad table and homemade breads and soups. Each meal is an "eat-as-much-as-you-like" affair, and the Saturday night buffet is popular. Picnic lunches are available daily. Guests are requested not to bring alcoholic beverages into the dining rooms or lounges. Guests may, however, have their own liquor in their bedrooms.

Accommodations: 14 rooms, 14 cottages, all with private bath.
Driving Instructions: Take Route 28 or 30 to Blue Mountain Lake which is about 100 miles northwest of Albany.

HEMLOCK HALL

P.O. Box 114, Blue Mountain, NY 12812. 518-352-7706. *Innkeeper:* L. Robert Webb. Open May 15 to October 15.

Hemlock Hall Lodge was built in 1898 and is a handsome, rustic mountain lodge with a large porch. Perched above Blue Mountain Lake, the lodge offers a full assortment of waterfront recreational activity including swimming, fishing (bass, rainbow, and native trout), canoeing, rowing, and sailing. There are also a number of self-guiding nature trails that depart from points near the lodge to hidden interior ponds or scenic lookouts. At the lakefront is a covered dockside pavilion. In addition to the innlike accommodations within the lodge itself there is also a small (four-unit) motel structure as well as ten cottages for those seeking more seclusion.

Meals at Hemlock Hall are simple, filling, American-style, single-entrée affairs. Typical main courses include roast lamb, roast pork, fricasseed chicken, corned beef, haddock, ham, turkey, and roast beef. The New England boiled dinner — corned beef and cabbage — is a specialty served every Thursday. The lodge is recommended by a number of travel associations, and advance reservations are almost always necessary. All in all, this is a cozy, rustic, and hospitable place to stay.

Accommodations: 24 rooms, 21 with private bath. *Pets:* Not permitted. *Driving Instructions:* The village of Blue Mountain Lake is located at the intersection of routes 28, 28N, and 30, about 100 miles northwest of Albany. From that intersection, continue north on 28N for ¾ mile. Watch for the lodge sign on the left. The lodge is about 1 mile down a private road along the north shore of Blue Mountain Lake.

Blue Mountain Lake is a tiny village in the middle of the extraordinarily beautiful lakes district of the Adirondack region. There are more than 2.5 million acres of Forest Preserve lakes and mountains in this area. The *Adirondack Museum* offers exhibits on logging, ice cutting, lodgings, and transportation (the surry buckboard that carried Teddy Roosevelt on his ride to the presidency is here), and more. A recent exhibit was called "Adirondack Woods and Waters" and is touted as the only recreationally themed display in a U.S. museum. In all there are exhibits in about twenty buildings.

HULBERT HOUSE

106 Main Street, Boonville, New York 13309. 315-942-4318. *Innkeepers:* Mary and Henry Daskiewich. Open all year except Election Day, Christmas Eve, and Christmas.

The Hulbert House is an attractive building on Main Street in Boonville, a quiet little northern New York town. The hotel was built in the early nineteenth century out of Black River limestone and local lumber, including hand-hewn maple and cherry paneling inside. A third story and an additional 30 feet were added to the hotel in 1839. The front of the building has a broad, handsome, two-story balconied portico supported by heavy columns of limestone, which in more recent years have been encased in wood. Post riders carrying the mail from Utica to the northern outposts stopped here, as did the Holland Company stagecoaches. The horses were changed while passengers stretched their legs and had drinks and food at the tavern bar. The hotel became even busier in the later nineteenth century when the Black River canal was opened and the Black River Railroad was completed. Boonville was the northern terminus of the railroad. In 1861, Colonel Charles Wheelock and his troops left from the Hulbert House and returned after the war for a reunion, bringing with them the regiment's flag, which had been presented to them when they left. The hotel register in the old lobby still bears the names of many distinguished guests, including General Ulysses S. Grant, Franklin D. Roosevelt, Horace Greeley, William Cody, and Thomas E. Dewey.

The Daskiewiches purchased the Hulbert House in 1964 and have renovated it and added a cocktail lounge named for the town's father, Gerret Boon. They also enlarged the kitchen, where Mary Daskiewich prepares the inn's lunches and dinners. The featured items on the menu are leg of lamb, ribs, and her special sauerbraten. The hotel has several dining rooms, including the Kortenaer Kitchen, which was once the kitchen, now a warm-hued room, its main feature being the old Dutch cooking fireplace with its large brick chimney. The Colonel Wheelock Room is a pleasant, more formal room where the troops returned after the Civil War. The Pioneer Bar has exposed carved limestone walls and murals depicting local historical events. Lunch and dinner are served here to the public and guests and breakfast to

guests on request only.

Accommodations: 14 rooms, 8 with private bath. *Pets:* Not permitted. *Driving Instructions:* Boonville is north of Utica on Route 12; or south from Watertown on Route 12. The hotel is on Main Street.

Camden, New York

THE VILLAGE INN

24 Mexico Street, Camden, NY 13316. 315-245-2182. *Innkeeper:* Donald Dunn. Open all year; the dining room open Tuesday through Sunday 11 A.M. to 10 P.M.

The Village Inn occupies the site of the 1796 homestead of Jesse Curtiss. The original wood-frame house was either torn down or moved from the property about a half-century later, and General Lyman Curtiss erected the present stone house in 1842. He was

president of Camden's first bank, and he commanded the home militia, the Camden Greys. The general died in 1868 at the age of seventy-six and was buried in the small cemetery directly across the street from his home, now the Village Inn.

Four dining rooms on the first floor of the inn have fabric wallpapers with damask prints. This paper is used throughout, with only a change in the color of the background from room to room. The maple dining tables were made locally by a small furniture factory. Among the menu's more than twenty entrées are the usual steaks, surf and turf, chicken, seafood dishes, lasagna, and spaghetti with meatballs and sausage, as well as the more elaborate lobster thermidor and scallops mornay. Dinners are served with soup or juice, salad, and potato. The menu also has a number of sandwiches for lunch or late-night lighter meals. The basement's Rathskeller bar has retained the inn's original stone walls except in the area around the dance floor. There innkeeper Donald Dunn has installed cherry paneling, which came from trees he felled and took to the sawmill himself. The Rathskeller remains open until 2 A.M. seven days a week.

On the second floor are the guest rooms. Each has its own bathroom, although two baths are accessible only from the hall. The Blue Room, furnished with antiques, has a black walnut high-back Victorian bed, a 9-foot gold-framed, marble-based mirror, and a cherry chest of drawers. The room is carpeted and has colored sheets and towels.

Accommodations: 4 rooms with private bath. *Pets:* Not permitted. *Driving Instructions:* Take Route 69 about 18 miles northwest of Rome.

THE INN AT THE SHAKER MILL

Cherry Lane, Canaan, NY 12029. 518-794-9345. *Innkeeper:* Ingram Paperny. Open all year.

The Inn at the Shaker Mill is, as the name implies, an inn housed in a classically simple 1824 Shaker gristmill. This beautiful building is constructed of cut fieldstone. Innkeeper Paperny purchased the building with the idea of using it for his experimental furniture workshop. A woodworker of some note, he designs and builds his furniture for many New York clients and guests at the inn.

The Shaker Mill is idyllic, set back from the Main Road on a small country dirt lane. A bubbling stream runs alongside, and at the rear of the building is a roaring waterfall — which formerly powered the mill. The interior is in keeping with the Shaker tradition — simple and functional. Several of the wideboard floors have been preserved, and others have been replaced with pegged-board floors. Paperny built a large circular staircase winding from the groundfloor dining area to the inn's second-floor lounge. He constructed an enormous, round open fireplace in the center of the lounge, where steaks are cooked to order. The furnishings of the rooms are spare, very comfortable, and all innkeeper-designed and -built.

The modern guest rooms in the mill are circled with Shaker-style peg railings on which are hung some of Ingram's specially designed lamps and unusual hanging nightstands. A sauna is available for guests — a nice place to meet and thaw out after a strenuous day of ice skating, skiing, or hiking. In addition to the sauna, guests will find a library well stocked with records, books, and magazines.

In the dining room, meals are served at Paperny's trestle tables and benches. The food is hearty and bountiful. The menu runs from a wide choice of unusual hot and cold appetizers, to a variety of homemade relishes served with the entrée, to a more than generous home-baked dessert served with gallons of good, steaming hot coffee. Wines and liquors are also available. Breakfast, lunch, and dinner are available to guests. Saturday evenings the dining room is open to the public as well.

A Shaker atmosphere pervades the inn and its setting. It is quite peaceful; the surrounding woods are lovely for hikes, and horses can

be hired at a nearby stable. In winter many good ski areas are just across the border in the Massachusetts Berkshires. The inn has its own skating pond.

Accommodations: 15 rooms, 13 with private bath. *Driving Instructions:* The inn is on Cherry Lane off Route 22, north of Queechy Lake. To reach Canaan, take exit B3 off I-90 and go north on Route 22. Or take the Taconic Parkway to Route 295 east, then 295 to Route 22 north.

Castile, New York

GLEN IRIS INN

Letchworth State Park, Castile, NY 14427. 716-493-2622. *Innkeeper:* Peter A. Pizzutelli. Open Easter through October.

Glen Iris Inn, in one of the East's most beautiful parks, overlooks the breathtaking 107-foot Middle Falls of the Genesee River. Glen Iris was the home of industrialist and philanthropist W. P. Letchworth from the 1850s until his death in 1910. When he died, he left to the State of New York more than 1,000 acres that encompassed more than 17 miles of the river, including three waterfalls.

Glen Iris, built in the 1820s, was enlarged in 1850 to serve as a tavern and again in 1859, when Mr. Letchworth bought it, into an impressive country estate. The inn's public rooms downstairs house a restaurant that features American cuisine emphasizing varied seafoods and veal dishes. An unusual paneled stairway leads to the small sunny and pleasant guest rooms. All are named for trees that grow in the park. Cherry Suite, by far the most formal and elegant, is booked years in advance. Guests can relax on the pillared portico lulled by the sound of the falls, or they may relax and read in the third-floor study with its vaulted beamed ceiling. Glen Iris is remarkable for its surroundings: the river, the falls, the deep canyons, and wildlife.

Accommodations: 21 rooms with private bath. *Pets:* Not permitted. *Driving Instructions:* From Route 20A at Warsaw, take Route 19 south to Route 19A and continue south on 19A to the entrance to Letchworth State Park.

Cazenovia, New York

Cazenovia, a pretty lakeside village in central upstate New York, is the home of Cazenovia Junior College. Settled in 1793 by John Lincklaen, the town has quietly prospered over the centuries. In 1807 John Lincklaen built a superb residence, *"Lorenzo,"* out of bricks fired on his property. The house has a commanding view of Cazenovia Lake and the surrounding hills. In 1968, it became a state historic site. Lorenzo is open as a museum from Wednesday through Saturday and sponsors a number of special events throughout the year.

Another building of architectural interest is the current site of the city government, the *Gothic Cottage*. The building is considered a romantic gem of the pre–Civil War era.

BRAE LOCH INN

5 Albany Street, Cazenovia, NY 13035. 315-655-3431. *Innkeeper:* H. Grey Barr. Open all year.

There is no mistaking it, Brae Loch is a tried and true Scottish inn. The building itself is a brown-shingled, bay-windowed, multigabled Victorian structure that is more than a century old. The interior has an unusual blend of Victorian and Scottish elements.

The inn has made its name primarily by its restaurant operation. There are six dining rooms, three on the main floor and three in the Rathskeller below. If you take the stairs to the lower level, you are greeted by a Victorian-style lounge complete with period lamps, furniture, and a gas fireplace. There are, in addition, a front dining room with two fireplaces, called the Grill Room, perhaps the most popular at the inn, where diners can watch the chef at work at the grill, and the back dining room with its pot-bellied stove, antiques, and stained-glass windows. Upstairs are a gift shop featuring Scottish goods; the Robert Burns Dining Room; and the Victorian Room, with its more formal setting. The Scottish theme is reinforced by the waitresses, who all wear kilts, and the inkeeper, who often wears a full-status Scottish uniform to work daily. A complimentary Continental breakfast is served to the inn's guests. The restaurant is closed December 24–25.

A winding staircase leads to the overnight accommodations upstairs. Here the choices are as varied as in the dining rooms. As examples, room 1 has two double beds, plaid curtains, a fireplace (nonfunctioning) with black marble mantel, antiques, and overstuffed chairs. Room 2 is the nicest, with hand-painted ceramic tile surrounding its fireplace (also nonworking), a window seat overlooking the lake, and a king-sized canopy bed. In all, three bedrooms have canopy beds.

The menu at dinner is large, relatively standard, and locally popular, featuring an assortment of steaks and chops, poultry, and seafood.

Accommodations: 9 rooms with private bath. *Driving Instructions:* Cazenovia is 18 miles east of Syracuse on Route 20. The inn is on Route 20 directly across from Cazenovia Lake, two blocks from the center of town.

Chautauqua, New York

ATHENAEUM HOTEL

Chautauqua, NY 14722. Summer phone: 716-357-5065; winter phone; 716-357-5635, ext. 245. *Innkeeper:* W. Thomas Smith. Open late June through late August.

The Athenaeum is a stately Victorian hotel built in 1881. Actually "stately" is a drastic understatement. This hotel is an enormous gingerbread building that brings home the true meaning of Victorian grandeur. The Athenaeum is a premium hotel here at the geographical and cultural center of the internationally famous Chautauqua Institution. It was built with the idea that hotel guests could mingle with guests of the institution appearing on the Chautauqua platform. The hotel boasts wonderfully wide verandas gracing the entire length of its front, overlooking the green, shaded lawn that slopes gently down to the lake shore. The building is crowned with a large rounded dome pierced with floor-to-ceiling and round windows a full four stories above the fantastic two-story glass entranceway. An elevator was installed in the hotel when the 48-room annex was constructed in 1924.

Inside the hotel is a charming high-ceilinged and high-windowed dining room that seats three hundred, with many tables providing a view of the lake. A spacious drawing room is filled with brightly upholstered wicker furniture and elaborate brass and crystal chandeliers, providing not only a beautiful lounging area where guests may relax and visit or read but also an impressive scene for receptions, recitals and meetings. The lobby has a wood-burning fireplace and is a favorite spot on cool summer evenings and rainy days. While public rooms and the main structure have been maintained in the style of the Victorian period in which it was built, the guest rooms have been modernized. Most of the hotel's rooms have tiled baths and showers, and the rooms are air conditioned.

Guests, Chautauqua residents, and visitors are served breakfast, lunch, and dinner in the elegant dining room. Liquor is not served in any of the Institution's hotels. The dinners consist of a choice from perhaps four entrées, such as broiled filet of snapper with lemon butter, ragout of beef with noodles, roast loin of pork, or perhaps chicken Antoinette — a breast of chicken and a slice of ham in supreme sauce. Included in the meal are two fresh vegetable choices, tossed salad, fresh hot rolls, relishes, soup or juice, and two desserts.

Accommodations: 168 rooms with private bath; several 2-bedroom suites are also available. *Pets:* Not permitted. *Driving Instructions:* From the north, east, or west, take I-90 to Westfield exit 60. Follow Route 17 to Mayville, then Route 394 for 3 miles south to the brick main gate entrance to Chautauqua Institution. From the south, take Route 394 north 16 miles from Jamestown to the main gate entrance.

ST. ELMO HOTEL

Chautauqua, NY 14722. 716-357-2285 or 665-4585. Open late June through August.

There is a tremendous range of accommodations offered on the Chautauqua Institution grounds. Because the Institution is a national landmark, most of the houses and hotels are maintained in their original turn-of-the-century forms. The St. Elmo is no exception. It is a fine, handsome country hotel that has the distinction of being the only one open all year. With nearly a hundred guest rooms the hotel is certainly no tiny, quaint country inn. It is, rather, a stately and attractive structure with a deep red clapboard exterior that sets off nicely the handsome small-paned windows and row of individual roofline dormers that spans the entire front of the building.

Inside, the feeling has been purposely maintained at the turn of the century. There are elaborate carved and paneled ceilings in many of the public rooms, and others have the original wainscoting. The furniture is a happy blend of hotel comfortable with amusing collections of wicker and, on the enclosed sunporch, of bent-bamboo lounging chairs. The dining room has its original spindle chairs. The paint is fresh, and the staff is loyal. Three employees have been in service for fifty years; some guests have returned for more than thirty summers. Guest rooms are decorated with original washstands, dressers, side tables, and wall-to-wall carpeting. The hotel overlooks Bestor Plaza, the center of the Institution.

The emphasis in food at the St. Elmo is on the good, old-fashioned, and homemade. There are roasts of beef, lamb, pork, chicken, or veal, as well as spare ribs, short ribs, and several fish choices. There is an abundance of vegetables (even a weekly Sunday night special of fried cornmeal mush), home-baked breads and desserts, and, all in all, more than plenty to eat. The dining room is capable of serving 450 diners daily. It does so every day of the ten-week summer season, testimony to its popularity.

Accommodations: 98 rooms, 37 with private bath. *Pets:* Usually not permitted. *Driving Instructions:* The entrance gates to the institution grounds are located on Route 374 in Chautauqua, about 16 miles northwest of Jamestown.

Clarence Hollow, New York

ASA RANSOM HOUSE

10529 Main Street, Clarence Hollow, NY 14031. 716-759-2315. *Innkeepers:* Judy and Robert Lenz. Open February through December except Fridays and Saturdays.

Asa Ransom House is an old brick-and-clapboard inn in the far-western corner of New York State. The inn is named for its builder, Asa Ransom, who purchased the land in 1799 from the Holland Land Company with the agreement that he would build and operate a tavern. It was a lonely wilderness with few settlers, but Asa set about building a two-story log tavern and, in the next few years, a sawmill and a gristmill, the first in Erie County. The exact date of the inn is uncertain, but Ransom built it about fifty years later (*ca.* 1853).

The original section of the inn houses the Tap Room, library, and gift shop, Sunshine Square. The Tap Room has a warm colonial atmosphere enhanced by the use of period oil lamps and shuttered windows. The library is reminiscent of "granny's parlor," complete with a fire in the Franklin stove, comfortable antique furniture, bookcases, and plenty of puzzles and table games. This is the perfect place to curl up with a good book. A guest in the library at the right time of day will be offered a hot cup of coffee or herb tea.

The guest rooms at Asa Ransom House are done with obvious care. The Gold Room has a lovely brick wall, the outside wall of the original building, with a hand-stenciled frieze on another wall. The Blue Room has a canopied double bed, and the Red Room sports an 1825 Cannonball double bed and a 1910 bathtub. The Green Room is spacious and has a view of the herb garden and lawns.

The dining rooms were added in 1975 with great care to maintain the nineteenth-century atmosphere. The Ransom Room is country formal, with high bay windows overlooking the lawns and herb garden. Smoking is not permitted in this dining room. Both rooms have fireplaces where roaring fires take the chill off on cool evenings. The Clarence Hollow Room is an informal, rustic dining room, with oak tables and wood floors.

The menu at the inn features New York State country cooking. There are delicious steaming kettle soups, fresh vegetables, plenty of homebaked rolls, breads, and muffins, and a good variety of meats, fish, and pot pies. Two favorites are Salmon Pond Pie, a deep dish of salmon, tomato, and vegetables with a topping of cheese pastry; and Smoked Corn Beef with apple raisin sauce. The beef is smoked in nearby Clarence Center. The inn also has daily blackboard specials, such as fricassee chicken served with granola biscuits or a fresh vegetable plate of four choice vegetables, a grilled tomato, artichoke heart, and raw milk cheese. The wine list is made up of New York State and nearby Ontario wines. Desserts are baked in the inn's kitchen and are brought around to the tables on big trays. Dinner is available to both guests and the public, but reservations should be made well in advance in view of the inn's popularity. A full country breakfast is served to guests only.

Accommodations: 4 rooms with private bath. *Pets:* Not permitted. *Driving Instructions:* Asa Ransom House is 15 miles east of Buffalo on Route 5, Clarence Hollow's Main Street.

THOUSAND ISLANDS INN

335 Riverside Drive, Clayton, 1000 Islands, NY 13624. 315-686-3030. *Innkeeper:* Allen Benas. Open late May through early October.

The Thousand Islands Inn, one of seven river-front Clayton inns when it was completed in 1897, captures the flavor of an era now gone by. It sits across the street from the St. Lawrence River and Seaway channel and is the only hotel to have survived the disastrous fires that claimed so many wood-frame buildings in the early part of this century. Activity at the inn centers around the bar and restaurant, which have both seen extensive renovation based on an early-American theme, with liberal use of barnboard providing the warm atmosphere. This is a particularly popular place for fishermen, who stay here in large numbers. The inn offers a special three-day-and-two-night package plan that includes fishing from one of the eight boats of the inn's fleet. The inn provides all meals, lodging, two full days of fishing, plus bait and tackle. Party boats for drift-fishing can also be obtained.

Throughout the season, the restaurant at the inn offers evening meals featuring steaks, chops, and a large selection of seafoods. Both the lounge and the dining room overlook the river. The guest rooms were recently modernized, and the atmosphere here reminds one more of a lodge than of an inn.

Accommodations: 17 rooms, 13 with private bath. *Driving Instructions:* Clayton is located at the intersection of Routes 12 and 12E at the St. Lawrence River.

Clinton, New York

THE CLINTON HOUSE RESTAURANT AND INN

21 West Park Row, Clinton, NY 13323. 315-853-5555. *Innkeeper:* Robert Hazelton. Open all year.

The Clinton House Inn sits at one corner of a town common. Formerly the Alexander Hamilton Inn, it was the elegant home of the town lawyer and his wife in the nineteenth century. Today it is a restaurant with guest rooms. The two large old parlor-sitting rooms are now dining rooms, as is the original dining room behind them. A large glassed-in porch, also a dining room, was added. The menu features veal dishes from each region of Italy. There are also beef, chicken, and fish entrées, most with an Italian flavor. Fridays are fish days.

The guest rooms retain their period decor, but carpets, television, and air conditioning have been added. The front room has a black marble fireplace and a view of the common. There is one other room with a fireplace, and one spacious room with an enormous bathroom that has floor-to-ceiling windows.

Accommodations: 5 rooms with private bath. *Driving Instructions:* Clinton is 10 miles south of the New York State Thruway—exit 31 (Utica) or exit 32 (Westmoreland).

Cold Spring, New York

HUDSON HOUSE

2 Main Street, Cold Spring, NY 10516. 914-265-9355. *Innkeeper:* Mary Pat Bevis. Open all year except January.

When we first saw the Hudson House, in late 1981, a major renovation was under way that involved hoisting up the building, stone walls and all, and constructing a new, higher foundation designed to withstand the occasional overflow of the Hudson River, just a few feet away. When we returned, in late 1982, a delight awaited us.

The inn's first floor is devoted to dining and living rooms where wideboard pine floors, wainscoting, decorative quilted appliqués, paddle fans, and pine furniture are the rule. In the dining room one may sit at calico-covered tables and gaze out at the river and the nearby park and bandstand. In summer, dining is extended to the inn's broad porch. Evening offerings include country-cured salmon and Back Roads bean pot with smoked salmon as starters and charbroiled chicken, country stew of pork and rabbit, hominy soufflé with sausages, and charbroiled beefsteak among several entrées.

Paddle fans are also used in the two floors of guest rooms above, including the six rooms that face the river. Beds run from brass to pine to iron to oak, and accessories include quilted wall hangings, decorative tinwork, and primitive pine bureaus, desks, and armoires.

Accommodations: 15 rooms with private bath. *Driving Instructions:* Take Route 9D to Cold Spring. In town, Main Street is split by the railroad. Bear left over the bridge to the continuation of Main Street and Hudson House.

Cooperstown, New York

COOPER INN

Chestnut Street, Cooperstown, NY 13326. 607-547-2567. *Innkeeper:* John N. Watt. Open Memorial Day through late October. In the heart of Leatherstocking country stands the Cooper Inn, named for America's first important novelist. It is the annex of Cooperstown's famous Otesaga Hotel, a country-estate resort on the south shore of Lake Otsego, the "glimmerglass" described by James Fenimore Cooper in *The Deerslayer*. The Cooper Inn was built as a private estate in the mid-nineteenth century. The brick home stands amid large shade trees and evergreens, and its wide front steps are flanked by stone tubs filled with geraniums and other summer blooms. Guests are deposited at the entrance by a sweep of circular drive. The Cooper, extensively restored and remodeled, is today a very attractive inn furnished throughout with reproduction eighteenth-century antiques and many authentic period pieces. The décor of the lobby, which sets the theme and atmosphere of the interior, is that of a home of a bygone era. The parlor just off the foyer offers guests a comfortable place to visit or read in pleasant surroundings. Beyond the lobby's front desk is the stairway leading to the inn's guest rooms, each of which is done up with period décor and reproduction antiques.

Guests are offered a light Continental breakfast during the peak of the summer season from late June to Labor Day. Other times and for all other meals, everyone is welcome to dine at the Otesaga Hotel, a block and a half away. The Otesaga, the grande dame of this historic lakeside town, was built as a palatial summer resort in the early 1900s. There was excellent rail service to the hotel, and it was also the perfect spot to motor to in that latest of fashionable acquisitions — the touring car. The hotel has been extensively restored and redecorated, its grounds well landscaped. The Otesaga may be even more luxurious today than it was when it opened in 1909. The furnishings then may have been of excellent quality, but the rooms appear to have been rather austere, an observation based on old photos taken for the July 16, 1909, edition of *The Otsego Farmer*. Today, the public rooms are carpeted and furnished throughout with period antiques and reproductions. Groupings of upholstered chairs and couches around fireplaces, brass chandeliers, and dashes of color from the many fresh flower arrangements make for a most enjoyable atmosphere. The main dining salon is a large affair with crystal chandeliers, fluted columns, ornate plaster work, and dark red swags on the many floor-to-ceiling windows. The public rooms at the Otesaga are available to guests of the Cooper Inn, as is the resort complex with its wide variety of outdoor recreational activities. The lake offers water sports and sightseeing. The Otesaga has a golf course at its doorstep, and there is a heated swimming pool between the lake and the hotel. Drinks and luncheon buffets are served at the poolside patio and on the terrace overlooking the lake.

A stay at the Cooper Inn combines the best of two worlds: quiet rooms in a smaller-inn setting; and the entertainment and resort facilities of a large full-service resort.

Accommodations: 32 rooms, 20 with private bath. *Driving Instructions:* Cooperstown is in central New York State, 70 miles west of Albany. It is on Route 80 and 28 at the south end of Lake Otsego. The inn is just a block and a half from the Otesaga Hotel on the lake.

THE HICKORY GROVE INN

Route 80 at Six Mile Point, Cooperstown. Mailing address: R.D. 2, Box 898, Cooperstown, NY 13326. 607-547-8100. *Innkeepers:* Polly and Jim Renckens. Open April 15 through October 31.

Jim and Polly Renckens are truly in love with their inn and derive endless pleasure from it. An inn has to be nice when the people who run it care so much. Hickory Grove Inn was built as a stagecoach stop in the early 1800s by the Van Ben Schoten family. A popular stop for travelers going from Cooperstown to the Cherry Valley Turnpike, the inn overlooks the southern tip of Otsego Lake, and, in the nineteenth century, the big lake steamboats stopped at the landing so passengers could dine at the inn. In 1865, the coaching tavern was expanded to include another dining room, two guest rooms, and an upstairs ball-room which was later converted to guest rooms. The guest rooms are individually decorated and have coordinated sheets and towels. Two overlook the lake and contain Victorian antiques, including big, high-headboard bedsteads. One room even has old nightshirts and a chamber pot and another has an old-fashioned featherbed.

The lounge downstairs features an 1865 wood-burning stove, a working player piano, old farm implements, and antique advertising art. The entire inn is filled with unusual antiques and collectibles. The oldest dining room, with its wide-pineboard floors and Early

American wallpaper, has a collection of "flo-blue" plates, old baby carriages, paintings by Sylvia Springer, butter churns, and more. In the candlelit front dining room there are always fresh flowers on the tables, and on chilly days a fire in the fireplace warms the room. In 1963 a large dining room was added to the lake side of the inn and is now lighted by wagon-wheel lamps and by the many windows overlooking the lake and fountain with its little stone ducks, frogs, and deer. The front porch has comfortable old furniture where guests can sit and have a drink before dinner.

The Hickory Grove menu features traditional inn fare with a few surprises, such as shrimp tempura and the specialty — pork chops with apple dressing and apple muffins. Guests receive a complimentary breakfast of coffee, sweet rolls, and fresh fruit.

Accommodations: 4 rooms with shared bath. *Pets:* Not permitted. *Driving Instructions:* The inn is 6 miles north of Cooperstown on Route 80.

TUNNICLIFF INN

34–36 Pioneer Street, Cooperstown, NY 13326. 607-547-9611. (taproom: 607-547-9860). *Innkeeper:* Magdalene Frank. Open all year.

Magdalene, John, and Ann Frank bought and restored the Tunnicliff Inn in 1927. Although John and Ann are since deceased, Magdalene continues as proprietress of this old-fashioned European-style in-town hotel. Built in 1802, the three-story brick inn retains many architectural elements of the early building. In the basement is the taproom dubbed "The Pit" by British troops occupying the building during the War of 1812. The original Dutch-oven fireplace survives there, although its original function as inn's the sole cooking facility has long since been replaced by a more modern kitchen.

Interestingly, Magdalene is almost more proud of what the inn doesn't have than of what it has. There is, she points out, no air conditioning, no swimming pool, and never a food served that has additives. What she does offer is a daily luncheon special reflecting her family's insistence on high-quality "good home cooking." It might be her meat loaf or perhaps a roast turkey with all the fixings; every item will be made from scratch from the starting soup to the closing pie or cake. In the evening the dining room is available only for special parties, weddings, or meetings.

Modernization is most evident in the guest rooms; each now has its own bathroom. Several bedrooms connect and are particularly suitable for families. Others are furnished with antiques, and some have fireplaces, although they may not be lighted because of insurance regulations. But the lobby and dining room fireplaces as well as the Dutch-oven fireplace in The Pit all do still function. The public rooms display the paintings of local artists. All in all, this small, family-run hotel could as easily be in a small European village as in upstate New York.

Accommodations: 22 rooms with private bath. *Driving Instructions:* Take Route 28, 80, or 205 to Cooperstown. The hotel is in town.

Corning, New York

ROSEWOOD INN

134 East First Street, Corning, NY 14830. 607-962-3253. *Innkeepers:* Winnie and Dick Peer. Open all year.

Rosewood was built in 1860 in the Greek Revival style. Because it was near the hospital, it was frequently the home of doctors practicing there. In the early years of this century, the wife of one such doctor decided that she and her husband were unhappy living in a house that looked so much like others on the block, so she had it remodeled in the Tudor style it retains today.

Rosewood's guest rooms are furnished in period antiques. The Herman Melville Room, for example, has an 1860 marble-topped dresser, carved pineapple twin beds, assorted whaling prints, and a model of the *Charles Morgan* whaling ship. The Jenny Lind Room has a spool bed bearing her name and various memorabilia relating to her visit to this country and Canada.

At the top of the stairs is the Cooper Sitting Room, which has three Cooper antique rocking chairs and a television for the use of guests. Breakfast is served downstairs in the paneled dining room. Rosewood is within walking distance of all Corning attractions.

Accommodations: 5 rooms, 3 with private bath. *Driving Instructions:* The inn is one block south of Route 17 between Chemung and Wall streets.

Dover Plains, New York

OLD DROVERS INN

Old Drovers Inn Road, Dover Plains, NY 12522. 914-832-9311. *Innkeeper:* Travis Harris III. Open all year except three weeks in December. Closed Tuesdays and Wednesdays.

Ask almost anyone to name a perfectly restored early American inn, and the chances are that they will include the Old Drovers Inn. Somehow, the Old Drovers is everyone's idea of a country inn carried to perfection. Built in 1750, the inn has been carefully restored to surpass even its original furnishings. Indeed, its original trade was with a group of rough-and-ready fellows who were hired to drive the cattle and swine raised by New England farmers to the markets in New York City. The drovers, who moved their stock from inn to inn along the old post roads, gave the inn its name. A bumptious crowd who liked good rum, they came to favor those inns that could provide the best distillate and good victuals.

Today, the drovers are gone, but the good victuals remain. The menu for each day is displayed on a blackboard and reflects the very finest, freshest ingredients obtainable locally or from the best of New York's markets. All service is à la carte. Consider starting your meal with the Old Drovers cheddar soup or any of several other special potages, pâtés, or equally enticing appetizers. Then comes the choice of entrée. House specialties include partridge with stuffing, prime sirloin steaks, Indian curries with assorted chutneys, steak and kidney pie, double-cut lamb chops, and the pièce de résistance—a locally grown whole baby pheasant, roasted in Burgundy and carved at the table. Assorted desserts and tea or coffee follow if you have a particle of room left.

The taproom is one of the East's most lovely dining rooms. Here are the heavy beams and lovely paneling of all of our dreams. Each table is set with a hand-etched glass shade surrounding a single candle. It was on this very spot that the drovers drank their tankards of ale and rum more than two hundred years ago. The romance continues today. Upstairs is the more formal Federal Room, with its highly polished mahogany tables and Georgian silver. Guests enjoy their breakfasts here, and the room is often the scene of private dining parties. The room is decorated with murals painted in 1941 by Edward Paine and depicting area landmarks such as the Roosevelt mansion in Hyde Park, the turrets of West Point, and the Old Drovers Inn itself.

There are only three bedrooms available for overnight guests. Each is a jewel, with lovely antique furnishings, fourposter beds, beautiful quilts, and fires in the bedroom fireplace. All in all, a visit to the Old Drovers is a special experience. Some of our friends have felt that staying here is a little like being in a museum. If you want to step back into history, the Old Drovers is for you.

Accommodations: 3 rooms with private bath. *Pets and Children:* Not permitted. *Driving Instructions:* The inn is about 75 miles from New York City on Route 22, three miles south of Dover Plains.

Dover Plains is a small village (population 950) about 25 miles east of Poughkeepsie and near the Connecticut border, in a lovely rural area with no tourist attractions as such, other than the surrounding scenic beauty. It is within an hour's drive of Hyde Park, the Vanderbilt Mansion, West Point, and many other historic attractions of the *Hudson Valley Region* as well as those of the neighboring Connecticut countryside.

BIG MOOSE INN

Big Moose Lake, Eagle Bay, NY 13331. 315-357-2042. *Innkeepers:* Doug and Bonnie Bennett. Open all year, except Monday and Tuesday during the fall and spring.

The Big Moose Inn is a simple rustic lodge on the shores of Big Moose Lake. The mountainous surroundings are picturesque, and whitetail deer are familiar residents in these parts. The inn, built in 1903, originally served guests who would arrive by train for their summer vacations. The old railroad line is being restored in connection with the 1980 Olympics to be held at Lake Placid. Transportation will be provided from the train depot to the inn. Big Moose Lake became known as the setting of *An American Tragedy* and the movie based on that Dreiser novel, which was entitled *A Place in the Sun* and starred Elizabeth Taylor and Montgomery Clift.

Guests at Big Moose Inn should not expect a truly old-fashioned look. The dining room, for instance, has typical restaurant furniture, wall-to-wall carpeting, and a general "modernized" appearance. Many of the rooms have lovely views of Big Moose Lake with its resident flock of wild mallards.

In summer the favorite dining spot is out on the deck with its colorful umbrella tables overlooking the lake. Many guests arrive by boat, tie up at the inn's dock, and have dinner or cocktails. Dinners are selected from a menu that features many traditional beef, chop, poultry, and seafood variants. There are some surprises including escargots as an appetizer and frogs' legs as an entrée. Desserts include a variety of homemade cakes and pies.

In winter snowmobilers and cross-country skiers are welcomed here, and the Bennetts have special snow season rates. Doug and Bonnie are congenial hosts who work hard to please their guests.

Accommodations: 16 rooms with shared baths. *Pets:* Not permitted. *Driving Instructions:* The inn is on Big Moose Road 5 miles north of Route 28 in Eagle Bay.

East Hampton, New York

East Hampton has the distinction of being called the most beautiful village in America. One walk down its main street will convince you of the aptness of this appellation. At one end of the street is the Old Hook Mill, a wind-powered gristmill dating from 1806 which is open during the summer months. At the other end is *Home Sweet Home*, the boyhood home of John Howard Payne, which inspired the song of the same name. Its small but excellent collection of Wedgwood, pewter, and lusterware can be viewed by the public during the summer and on a limited schedule during the winter months. (Because of the museum's limited space, groups are requested to make an advance appointment. Call Mrs. Avril Geus, the curator, at 516-324-0713.) Behind the museum is a meticulously-restored, early Long Island windmill. *Clinton Academy* has, for a small museum, one of the best local history collections, with some outstanding examples of early furnishings, tools, costumes, and artifacts dating back to the seventeenth century. It is open summers only. *Guild Hall* is a local art museum and center for the performing arts that has exhibits, theatrical productions, and special classes the year round.

HEDGES HOUSE

74 James Lane, East Hampton, New York. Mailing address: P.O. Box 1553, East Hampton, NY 11937. 516-324-7100. *Innkeepers:* Kenneth Baker and Richard Spencer. Open March 15 through December 31.

Hedges House stands just off the Montauk Highway welcoming travelers entering East Hampton. Not long ago Hedges House offered only a shabby welcome, hardly fitting for one of America's most beautiful villages. Now, thanks to the extraordinary efforts of Kenneth Baker and Richard Spencer, Hedges House has been transformed into an elegant country inn and restaurant.

The innkeepers spent a full year totally restoring the inn inside and out. The grounds are lushly planted with ornamental shrubbery, flowers, and shade trees. Inside, the guest rooms upstairs are bright and airy, with white shutters at the windows and carpeted floors. The beds are covered with attractive puffs, and each room has antique furnishings. Ken spends much of his free time checking the multitude of

antique shops in the area for suitable pieces to augment those already there. Most of the rooms are air-conditioned, and all have tiled baths. A favorite guest room on the second floor is all white from the dust ruffles to the window shutters; another, on the third floor, has sloping eaves.

The ground floor of Hedges House is given over to an attractive reception room and the inn's two dining rooms, which constitute En Brochette, the Eastern counterpart of the innkeepers' successful Beverly Hills restaurant. Among the skewered entrées are filet mignon with mushroom caps, marinated shrimp, and a vegetarian platter of freshly steamed vegetables "en brochette." A number of other, nonskewered dishes are offered regularly.

Hedges House stands on land settled in 1652 by some of the first settlers in the Hamptons, the Hedges family. They built the earliest section of the inn in 1774 and retained it until 1923. Today the house is listed in the National Register of Historic Places. The inn is a pleasant walk from the beach and from the center of the village.

Accommodations: 14 rooms with private bath. *Driving Instructions:* Take Route 27 into the center of East Hampton. From the traffic light, drive straight ahead about 100 feet to the inn.

THE HUNTTING INN

94 Main Street, East Hampton, NY 11937. 516-324-0410. *Innkeeper:* Bruce Bozzi. Open March through October or November.

Nathaniel Huntting began building his home on Main Street in 1699. Half a century and several additions later, his wife turned the home into a "Publick House," and it has been accepting guests ever since. During the Revolutionary War the inn was the only neutral meeting place on the South Fork of Long Island. After several recent changes of ownership, the Huntting Inn was finally purchase by the proprietors of the Palm Restaurant in New York, who completely renovated its public rooms as part of the conversion of the Huntting restaurant to a branch of the Palm. The excellence of the Palm is the reason why most local people are familiar with the Huntting Inn. In keeping with Palm standards established more than half a century ago, only enormous portions (a full pound of filet mignon or a 4- to 5-pound lobster, for example) are served. In addition to the steak and lobster specialties, which are renowned, the Palm prepares five versions of veal scallopine, several poultry dishes, and an assortment of chop and seafood dishes. One of the most pleasant spots to eat at the Palm at Huntting Inn is the glassed-in front porch, where large-bladed paddle fans provide a Casablancan atmosphere.

Many of the guest rooms have brass or iron bedsteads, and all sport fluffy quilts and dust ruffles. The baths are provided with special soaps, and Godiva chocolates are regularly placed on pillows in the bedrooms. One of the nicest is room 111, with its exposed hand-hewn and hand-planed beams, old-fashioned wallpaper, and traditional furnishings. Elaborate gardens are planted with thousands of bulbs and are a riot of color in warm months.

Accommodations: 26 rooms, 22 with private bath. *Pets:* Not permitted. *Driving Instructions:* Take Route 27 to the center of East Hampton, where it becomes Main Street.

THE MAIDSTONE ARMS

207 Main Street, East Hampton, NY 11937. 516-324-5006. *Innkeepers:* Rita M. and Gary D. Reiswig. Open all year.

The Maidstone Arms is a large inn overlooking East Hampton's village pond. In winter the pond has skaters gliding past the Christmas tree in its center; in summer it reflects the centuries-old gravestones of a cemetery at the water's edge. The Maidstone's foundations were part of a tannery that operated here in the seventeenth century, serving one of the oldest villages on Long Island. The main house was built by the Osbourne family in 1750, and a large addition was put on at the turn of this century. The house remained in the family for many years; in the middle of the Victorian era they converted it to an inn.

East Hampton maintains an understated quality with its substantial time-softened shingle "cottages," and the Maidstone Arms is no exception. As you enter the inn, you are drawn to the right into the bright, sun porch–living room or to the left into the older part of the inn where the bar and future dining room are located. The sun porch has white wicker furniture (even wicker lamps). A library nook in this room has a large selection of books and a Noble wood stove to provide warmth. Breakfasts are served on this porch each morning on rattan trays bearing coffee, juice, and croissants or brioches. In the evening, liqueurs are served by the fire in the paneled bar. The inn's restaurant is run by Chef Morris Weintraub, well known locally for his Continental cuisine. The veal Orloff and Long Island duckling are not to be missed. Seafood from nearby waters is also featured in the antique-filled dining room.

Guest rooms at the Maidstone Arms, found on three floors, show a great deal of individuality in arrangement and décor. Room 42, a first-floor room facing the street, has its own small glassed-in sun porch and is furnished in wicker. Another room (number 20) has a nonfunctional fireplace, a quilt on the carved Victorian bed, and a comfortable wing chair. Rooms on the third floor are air-conditioned and spatter-painted floors are the rule as is an interesting floral wallpaper with a charcoal background. Other rooms have small-figure print wallpaper with various pictures on the walls, and views of either the pond or the lawn to the rear. The inn's foyer has been newly wallpapered, and Oriental carpets cover the hallway and office areas. In summer, guests frequently relax on lawn furniture or play croquet.

Accommodations: 21 rooms, 13 with private bath. *Pets:* Not permitted. *Driving Instructions:* Take Route 27 into East Hampton, where it becomes Main Street.

1770 HOUSE

143 Main Street, East Hampton, NY 11937. 516-324-1770. *Innkeepers:* Sidney and Miriam Perle. Open all year as a rule, but in the winter call to be sure.

For years the old 1770 House had been allowed to deteriorate. Then, in 1977, Sid and Mim Perle left their western Long Island businesses (he had been a retailer of women's sportswear and she the owner of a cooking school and catering service) and bought the inn. Thus began one of the nicest renovations of a village inn that we have seen.

You have but to enter the front door of the inn to realize that you are in a fine Long Island inn, steeped in history and more gracious now than ever before. To the right is an intimate library, the heart of the house, with a fireplace that has an old brass firescreen and andirons. The surrounding wall paneling was buried under several layers of paint until many hours of hard work revealed the original pecan-wood panels. One corner of this room contains the upstairs bar with its high bentwood bar stools. This room, like all the others in the inn, is filled with lovely antiques from the Perles' extensive collection. As the visitor passes from room to room he will be treated to an array of antique clocks, Rogers statuary, and early chairs and beds. Where it has been necessary to use reproductions, their relative newness often goes unnoticed.

To the left are the two dining rooms with ten tables. The adjoining rooms have a light, airy feeling. The color scheme is crisp brown and white set off by the natural oak tables. There are stained-glass windows at either side of the room and fresh flowers on all the tables.

Mim Perle takes more joy in food and her cooking than almost anyone else we know. Her menu changes weekly and is a wonderful sampling of her Cordon Bleu training. The dinner is always prix fixe. When we last ate there we had a choice of six appetizers, including mozzarella en carozza, lobster quiche, Oriental crabmeat salad, and scallops vinaigrette. This was followed by choice of swordfish Chinois en papillote, Shrimpo Fra Diavolo, lemon walnut chicken, salmon in struedel, and three other entrées. The desserts were an assortment of rich cakes, mousses, and a banana dream cream. Mim's personal favorite dessert is her puffed crepes with honey butter. Every item on the menu is prepared by Mim in her extraordinary kitchen, a chef's dream, which has a cathedral ceiling with exposed beams.

Equally romantic is the eighteenth-century taproom in the cellar of

the old inn. Two rooms here have exposed beams and brick walls, and there is a small bar in the corner. The walls are decorated with the Perles' collections of advertising art. Popular as a congenial drinking spot, the taproom is also used for dinner service when the inn is crowded. In the winter the taproom is used more frequently for dining before the 5-by-7-foot colonial beehive fireplace with its 3-foot-high andirons and iron kettles hanging from the fireplace brackets.

The 1770 House offers a total of six bedrooms, all filled with more of the Perles' antiques. Four of the bedrooms are upstairs in the main part of the house and are reached by the central stairway, with an old grandfather clock on the landing. The remaining two rooms have private entrances but are attached to the inn itself. All rooms have private baths and are papered with appropriate prints. All have elegant Dior sheets and fluffy towels, and four have canopy double beds. Each has its own particular happy details: In one there is a working fireplace, another has a working brass railroad lamp, a third has a bank of leaded glass windows, and another has stained glass in the bathroom.

Accommodations: 6 rooms with private bath. *Pets:* Not permitted. *Children:* Under twelve, not permitted. *Driving Instructions:* The inn is in the center of the village on the west side of Route 27, across from Guild Hall and next to Clinton Academy.

THE REDCOAT'S RETURN

Dale Lane, Elka Park, NY 12427. 518-589-6379. *Innkeepers:* Peggy and Tom Wright. Open from May 31 to November 1 and November 15 through March 31.

The Redcoat's Return, a popular English-style country inn and restaurant in the heart of the Catskill Mountains, sits at 2,200 feet elevation, overlooking beautiful forests, grassy meadows, and Schoharie Creek, which runs right by the inn. The setting is impressive, with the age-old Catskills rising up all around the inn's property. The four-story white clapboard building was built in 1910 during the Catskills' "summer boarding house" boom. It remained as a summer inn (with an almost ten-year rest when the summer tourist trade dwindled after World War II) until Tom and Peggy Wright took over the business in 1972. Armed with lots of wonderful ideas, a love of good food, and boundless energy and elbow grease, they transformed the old summer boarding house into a cozy (winterized!) English inn. The entire place has been carefully decorated with antiques, old paintings, and comfortable old furnishings, all of which contribute to the look and atmosphere of merrie olde England. The returning Redcoat for which it is named, by the way, is Tom, former denizen of the British Isles and former chef of Cunard's *Queen Mary*. Both Tom and Peggy are refugees from the New York City rat race. The other popular members of the innkeeping team are Rex, an Irish Setter, and Rover, a big Collie.

All guest rooms at the Redcoat's Return have recently been redecorated with comfortable, homey antiques, a variety of old beds and washstands, and prints and paintings on the walls. Downstairs the heart of the inn is the Pub-lounge, where guests can curl up in front of a fire under the watchful eye of a large moose head on the fieldstone fireplace chimney. There is also an attractive reading room where one can bring one of the Wrights' many books, chosen from the extensive scholarly collection of more than two thousand volumes lining the library-*cum*-dining room walls.

Tom is an excellent cook. In addition to his stint on the *Queen Mary* he apprenticed at London's Dorchester House. The restaurant carries on the English tradition here: the popular entrées include

steak-and-kidney pies, English fish'n chips, hearty prime ribs with Yorkshire pudding, curries, fresh fish, and roast duckling. British ales and beers are specialties at the bar, which is ably tended by Peggy. Wines and liquors are also available. Dinner is served to guests and the public daily except Thursdays, when the restaurant is closed in the evening. Guests also receive a hearty country breakfast of eggs, English jams and muffins, griddle cakes—you name it.

The inn adjoins the Catskill Game Preserve with its more than 250,000 acres. Marked hiking trails lead from the inn's door up the mountains to magnificent views of the Hudson Valley below. The fields and forests around the inn are also fine for quiet walks, and Schoharie Creek provides excellent trout fishing. The porches are perfect places for just plain relaxing and enjoying the scenery, as is the gazebo out by the croquet lawn.

Accommodations: 14 rooms, 7 with private bath. *Pets:* Not permitted. *Driving Instructions:* Take Route 23A to Tannersville (about 16 miles west of Catskill). Turn south at the light and follow signs to Police Center (4 miles). Turn right on Dale Lane.

Garrison, New York

BIRD AND BOTTLE INN

Route 9, Garrison, NY 10524. 914-424-3000. *Innkeeper:* Ira Boyar. Open all year except Mondays and Tuesdays November through March.

The Bird and Bottle Inn is but a short drive from Manhattan, set well back from the road in a pastoral setting. Here it is no trouble at all to put behind you immediately the bustle of city life just 50 miles away.

The inn looks as it must have looked two centuries ago, when it was known as Warren's Tavern. As you step down into the low-beamed tavern room itself, it is easy to conjure up images of the Revolutionary War soldiers who must have paused here for refreshment. Just down the hall is the inn's main dining room, where a fire is often blazing in the cooking hearth. The centerpiece of this room is a proud-looking stuffed pheasant with an accompanying bottle of wine, whence the inn's name arose.

Candelight dining at the Bird and Bottle Inn includes a number of offerings on a prix fixe menu, all of which are derived from classic European cooking traditions. A recent meal included trout smoked at the inn, country pâté, tournedos, and sautéed kidneys bordelaise. Pheasant, chicken breast, duckling, and several seafood dishes are menu regulars, and several desserts are available daily.

Upstairs are the expertly decorated guest rooms. The focal point of each is a canopied bed created through the skillful swagging of designer fabrics. The suite has a working fireplace presided over by a properly stern early-American primitive painting of a mother and daughter. Tiny-print wallpapers and antique furniture are found in each of the guest rooms. Just behind the inn are a burbling brook and a winding country gravel road that leads up a hillside past stone walls and handsome Colonial farmhouses.

Accommodations: 4 rooms with private bath. *Pets:* Not permitted. *Driving Instructions:* The inn is on Route 9, 8 miles south of I-84 and 8 miles north of Peekskill.

THE GOLDEN EAGLE INN

Garrison's Landing, NY 10524. 914-424-3067. *Innkeepers:* George and Stephanie Templeton. Open April through mid-January.

The Golden Eagle Inn stands in a parklike setting with views of the Hudson River and the distant Catskill Mountains. It was built in the 1840s to serve the Garrison's Landing railroad station and ferry dock. It began as the Garrison Hotel and was visited by many dignitaries, even queens and kings, who spent a restful night before crossing by ferry to West Point.

Today, the three-story brick hotel has been restored and refinished. The present innkeepers began the restoration in 1971, bringing a wealth of decorating talent and artists' skill to the job. Both had been in design in New York City—Stephanie Templeton as an interior designer and George as an industrial designer and a display specialist for a major New York department store. He is also known for his portraits of yachts, and he somehow manages to fit his artwork into the busy schedule of an innkeeper.

Each guest room here is done in a different color scheme, using old-fashioned wallpapers and many antiques. Some of George Templeton's original watercolors decorate the walls of these rooms and the lounge downstairs. Continental breakfast of fresh fruit, coffee or tea,

and perhaps a croissant or muffin with jams is served on the veranda, which has spectacular views, or in the Veranda Café in cool weather. The café is open to the public for lunch. The gallery-lounge is a favorite spot in which to gather for cocktails or conversation in the evening.

The riverside hamlet of Garrison's Landing is steeped in history. George Washington and his officers were rumored to have spent several nights with the "ladies" at the nearby Manderville House. The ferry-dock house is right next to the inn, and a rowboat and a canoe are to be found at the end of the inn's broad lawn, which runs down to the peaceful river. Nearby are West Point, Hyde Park, Sleepy Hollow, and many antique shops, art galleries, and Hudson Valley wineries.

Accommodations: 6 rooms, 4 with private bath. *Pets and Children:* Not permitted. *Driving Instructions:* Take Palisades Parkway to Bear Mountain Bridge. Cross bridge and take Route 9D to Route 403. From 403 take Route 14 to the inn.

Geneva, New York

THE COBBLESTONES

R.D. 2, Geneva, NY 14456. 315-789-1896. *Innkeepers:* Mr. and Mrs. Lawrence Gracey. Open all year.

The date stone over the main entrance of the Cobblestones indicates it was built in 1848 by T. Barron. This handsome home is an inspired example of Greek Revival architecture, with four large fluted columns and Ionic capitals. On either side of the central section are balancing wings with smaller versions of the columns. The entire place was constructed of lake-washed sandstone sorted for size and color. The cobblestone architecture is typical of this section of western New York, extending about 90 miles along the southern shore of Lake Ontario. Most of these cobblestone buildings were constructed during a thirty-year period between 1820 and 1850.

The Cobblestones is a guest house; it serves no meals. The furnishings are mostly antique with many Oriental rugs throughout. The Graceys will gladly suggest restaurants in the surrounding Geneva-Finger Lakes area.

Accommodations: 3 rooms with shared bath. *Pets:* Welcome. *Children:* Welcome. *Driving Instructions:* The New York State Thruway, exit 42 or 44, to Geneva. The Cobblestones is on the north side of Routes 5 and 20, about 3½ miles from Geneva.

THE INN AT BELHURST CASTLE

Lockland Road, Geneva, New York. *Mailing address:* P.O. Box 609, Geneva, NY 14456. 315-781-0201. *Innkeeper:* Robert J. Golden. Open March through December.

Belhurst Castle, a turreted Medina stone structure, was constructed from 1885 to 1889 by Mrs. Carrie Harron Collins, a descendant of Henry Clay's. The building was constructed, at a cost of $475,000, by fifty workmen including fourteen European woodcarvers using materials mostly imported from Europe. After Mrs. Collins's death the house was sold to Cornelius Dwyer, who converted the castle into a renowned restaurant and gambling casino. In fact, gambling continued at Belhurst until the U.S. Senate's Kefauver hearings in the early 1950s. When the castle was purchased in 1975 by its present owner, the restaurant operation was continued, but only recently has it been possible to spend the night in the restored upstairs guest rooms.

Great care has been used in renovating and furnishing these rooms. The Dwyer suite, for example, has a superb antique mahogany four-poster bed and complementing upholstered mahogany armchairs. The Reed Room features bird's-eye maple paneling laced with bamboo in an Oriental effect continued in the custom-made furnishings throughout the room.

Among Belhurst's notable features are its eight fireplaces. Each different, the mantles combine tilework and distinctive paneling. The center hall of the second floor has been furnished as a living room for overnight guests. An original ice-water spigot now dispenses chilled Chablis for houseguests.

This "Richardsonian Romanesque" castle is on 25 acres on a bluff overlooking Seneca Lake. A curved drive leads to the inn's entrance. The manicured grounds are dotted with well-kept shrubs and towering white and red oaks.

Belhurst's ambitious menu offers more than a dozen appetizers and a wide range of beef, veal, seafood, and poultry dishes.

Accommodations: 6 rooms with private bath. *Pets:* Not permitted. *Driving Instructions:* The inn is on Route 14, 3 miles south of Routes 2 and 5.

CEDAR HILL

Tice Hill Road, Ghent, NY 12075. 518-392-3923. *Innkeepers:* Stephen Richer and Kendra Smith. Open all year.

Cedar Hill began its life as a small farmhouse. From 1940 to 1950, Broadway playwright Larry Gelbart transformed it into a large country home with addition after addition. On 20 acres of rolling countryside, Cedar Hill is bordered by a white post-and-rail fence and a row of sentinel arborvitae. Reached by a dirt road in a secluded part of Ghent, the inn has two living rooms where guests may gather. The front room has a wood stove, a piano, upholstered chairs, and a couch. The larger living room has a cathedral ceiling with exposed beams, a fireplace, and a mixture of antiques (desk, bench, and chest) and more modern furnishings. The carpeted sunporch is furnished in wicker. The dining room, serving guests breakfast, lunch, and dinner as they desire, also has a beamed cathedral ceiling and a fireplace. Breakfast, included in the room rate, offers homemade granola bread, tomato preserves, and other natural foods. The culinary specialties here are gourmet dishes made with fresh natural ingredients. The innkeepers are interested in nutrition, and they sometimes offer special health programs.

Each guest room is different in color and furnishings. Beds range from twin to king-size and are tucked into the many different levels and angles of the house. Cedar Hill is an attractive yet unpretentious place where guests are likely to feel completely at home. A swimming pool and a pool house (with two bedrooms and an adjoining bath) are on the grounds. There is also a tennis court, and in winter, cross-country skiing is available on the property and on trails through the surrounding farmland and forests.

Accommodations: 9 rooms, 4 with private bath. *Pets:* Permitted only if small. *Driving Instructions:* Take the Taconic Parkway to Harlemville Road (between the Philmont-Harlemville and Chatham exits). Turn west and go 1.5 miles to Tice Hill Road.

Greenport, New York

TOWNSEND MANOR INN

714 Main Street, Greenport, NY 11944. 516-477-2000. *Innkeeper:* Alex Gonzalez. Open all year; restaurant closed December through March.

Townsend Manor Inn consists of four buildings that in many ways span the history of this seaside Long Island village. On 3 acres of lawn with large shade trees, Townsend Manor Inn is bordered by tree-lined Main Street on one side and the waterfront on the other. Its main building dates back to the booming days of the early nineteenth century, when whaling men would leave from Greenport or neighboring Sag Harbor on trips often lasting more than a year. A major shipbuilding port, Greenport was the scene of many thriving businesses. In 1835 a prosperous whaling captain named George Cogswell bought a parcel of waterfront land and built himself a residence that is today the main building at Townsend Manor Inn. In the columned building are the restaurants, cocktail lounge, and the parlor. The main dining room was also the original dining room of the house and retains its stained wide-board wainscoting with wallpaper over the chair rail and the original fireplace. There is the small Gold Dining Room in the former sitting room of the captain's house, as well as a recently added glassed-in patio dining room. The parlor has its original wide-board floor and a working fireplace. The interior of the Main House has been redecorated in the Early American theme with old-fashioned wallpapers and a predominantly gold and russet decor.

The menu at Townsend manor offers the major Long Island specialties — seafood and duckling — as well as a number of meat entrées.

Hotel rooms are in the separate Gingerbread House, Captain's House, and Waterfront Cottage. Gingerbread House, one of the finest Victorian buildings in the area, was erected in 1843 as a home for Grosvenor Adams, founder of the First National Bank of Greenport. The exterior was renovated to its present ornate Victorian appearance by Adams's daughter Sarah. One apartment in this building has the old Victorian woodwork, ornate trim, and retains the high ceilings and windows. However, most accommodations within Gingerbread House and Waterfront Cottage (erected in the early twentieth century) have been remodeled in more modern decor and furnishings. The Captain's House has five rooms furnished in a Colonial motif. There are private balconies that look out over the marina. All rooms have wall-to-wall carpeting, television, modern ceramic-tiled and wood-paneled bathrooms, and individually controlled air-conditioning and heat.

Recreational facilities at the inn include the pool and shuffleboard. Nearby is a championship eighteen-hole golf course where inn guests have reduced-fee privileges. The inn has its own full-service marina; riding, tennis, sailing, boating, fishing, and miniature golf are nearby.

Accommodations: 23 rooms with private bath. *Pets:* Not permitted. *Driving Instructions:* Take Route 25 or County Route 27 from Riverhead or Route 25 from the Orient Point Ferry to Greenport. The inn is on Main Street (Route 25), ½ mile north of the center of town.

Greenville, New York

GREENVILLE ARMS

Greenville, NY 12083. 518-966-5219. *Innkeepers:* Barbara and Laura Stevens. Open all year.

The Greenville Arms, built in 1890 by William Vanderbilt, is a handsome, ornate home with a single turret, a bay window, and porches that span two floors. Its grounds include 7 acres of lawns, a brook, quaint wooden bridges, gardens, and a swimming pool. The home itself is noted for its original chestnut woodwork, floor-to-ceiling brick fireplaces, and hardwood floors. Old clocks, bed warmers, pottery, and china adorn the walls, mantel, and cupboards. Tiffany-style lamps or Victorian chandeliers provide lighting in the public rooms. The inn maintains a library chock-full of books to read by the fireplace.

The Greenville Arms offers a total of twenty guest rooms, although in the winter some are not rented. Meals at the Greenville are served family style with a single entrée each evening. All include homemade breads and desserts. For dinner, reservations are required.

Accommodations: 20 rooms, 14 with private bath. *Pets:* Permitted only occasionally. *Driving Instructions:* From Catskill, take Route 23 west to Cairo bypass, then turn right on Route 32 north to Freehold and on to Greenville. Look on the west side of Route 32, just south of the traffic light.

Groton, New York

BENN CONGER INN

206 West Cortland Street, Groton, NY 13073. 607-898-3282. *Innkeepers:* Robert and Margaret Oaksford. Open all year; restaurant closed in January.

Benn Conger was the first president of the Corona Corporation, the company that gave Groton its first substantial industry, which survives today as the SCM Corporation. Conger's handsome mansion has been meticulously restored and is now a superb country inn and restaurant. On a quiet side street, it is surrounded by 3 acres of lawns.

Four separate dining rooms at the inn are noted for period reproductions of Chippendale and Windsor furniture and Palladian windows. The Blue Room, Conger's original dining room, has gold-trimmed wallpapered panels, a scroll chair rail, keyhole moldings, and corner cupboards. The Cantwell Room has a white marble fireplace, while the Conservatory has Palladian windows on three sides. Chef's specialties include chicken Sarrono, pork loin Normandy, tournedos Richelieu, and bay scallops with chervil sauce. Benn's Den, once the library, is now a service bar with an inviting fireplace.

The guest rooms are furnished primarily with antiques. One room has a ceiling fan; room 3, once the master bedroom, has a large private bath and dressing room. A full country breakfast, included in the lodging fee, is served in the Morning Room. The Benn Conger Inn is within an easy drive of the universities at Cortland and Ithaca.

Accommodations: 4 rooms, 2 with private bath. *Pets:* Not permitted. *Children:* Under twelve not permitted. *Driving Instructions:* Groton is on Route 38, 10 miles north of Dryden.

Hamilton, New York

COLGATE INN

On-the-Green, Hamilton, NY 13346. 315-824-2300. *Innkeeper:* John VanAmburgh. Open all year.

Hamilton is reminiscent of a New England college town with its village green and many colonial houses. An appropriate addition to this Currier and Ives setting is the Colgate Inn. Owned by the university, it has been a popular gathering spot for students and their parents as well as returning alumni since it was built in 1925. The Dutch colonial–style building, dominated by a two-story pillared porch, combines a partial stone facing with white shingles that rise to its gabled roof. Inside the inn, guests enter a large, old-fashioned lobby with tall, French door–style windows and floor-to-ceiling drapes. An open spiral stairway leads from the lobby to the upper two floors and their guest rooms.

The Salmagundi Room, the inn's main dining room, shares its name with the Colgate yearbook. The colonial-style room has wide-board pine floors and a large open-hearth fireplace. Its walls are paneled with wood, and iron wheel chandeliers hang from the beamed ceiling. The inn is especially proud of its roast prime rib, veal steak champignon, sea bass à la Russe, and baked stuffed shrimp maison. For many years the Colgate Inn has enjoyed local renown for its buffet-style Sunday brunch, which offers regulars like eggs Benedict, as well as such special treats as roast beef sliced at your table, hot cheese blintzes with blueberry sauce, fresh fruit salad, and the inn's unusual oatmeal salad.

The main cocktail lounge is called the 1840 Room, in honor of an important growth period in the history of both Colgate and Hamilton. The room has barn siding combined with a brick wall and is candlelit for quiet before- or after-dinner drinks. Downstairs, a second bar known as the Old Maroon is a popular gathering spot for students.

The guest rooms are on the upper two floors and were recently completely renovated; all are air-conditioned and contain color televisions and private bathrooms. Room décor was developed around the recently revived Hitchcock chair factory line of stenciled beds, chairs, rockers, and dressers.

Accommodations: 46 rooms with private bath. *Pets:* Not permitted. *Driving Instructions:* Take Route 128 about 5 miles south of Route 20 (turn south at Pine Woods).

High Falls, New York

THE DEPUY CANAL HOUSE
(AND BRODHEAD HOUSE)

Route 213, High Falls, NY 12440. 914-687-7700 or 7777. *Innkeeper:* John Novi. Brodhead House open daily all year for accommodations. The Depuy Canal House serves meals Thursday through Sunday.

These two inns are in separate buildings serving the separate functions of eating and sleeping, but they may be considered a single inn aptly run by John Novi. His Depuy Canal House established his fame as a restaurateur, and it is on this tavern that we must dwell. In fact, the following are John's own words, as appropriate as any we could have devised.

The Depuy Canal House "itself was established as a tavern in 1797 when it was built by Simeon Depuy, one of the foremost citizens of the small hamlet of High Falls. In the early 1820s an addition was put on the front of the structure which was reportedly used as a slave quarters and a storage area...

"In 1826 the tavern's business boomed with the opening of the Delaware and Hudson Canal which flowed right past the door of the tavern. Even today visitors can see the indentations in the corner of the house caused by ropes being dragged thousands of times over the stone as the barges were pulled up against the side of the canal to be unloaded at 'Dupuys.' Although the section of the canal that ran in front of the house wall filled in when Route 213 was constructed, Lock 16, situated directly behind the tavern, is still in good shape. After passing through a number of hands after the canal closed in 1898, John Novi bought the building in 1964 and four years later began the huge task of restoration.

"Since the Tavern's reopening, gourmet meals have been served to the public from old-fashioned hearts and flowers china placed on roofing slates. Six-course meals are served by candlelight in a leisurely, old world atmosphere. Herbs lie drying on an herb rack suspended over the fireplace while peppers and onions hang in clusters."

Many guests at the inn have driven there especially for its meals, of such quality that Craig Claiborne rated the Tavern with four stars, his highest accolade. Offerings vary each day but starters might include beignets, oysters Florentine, fava bean soup, eggplant and clam chowder, or any number of other less than frequently encountered beginnings to a fine meal. Entrées of the day could be striped bass, broiled fresh bass, mackerel, or other fish with any number of inventive sauces, roast beef, rack of lamb, stuffed partridge with ginger-walnut sauce, or rabbit Chinese-style as an entrée or in stir-fried bits as an appetizer. For the lucky few who make advance reservations, there are now three Victorian-style rooms in the restored 1879 Italianate Brodhead House just across the way.

Accommodations: 3 rooms with shared bath. *Pets:* Not permitted. *Driving Instructions:* Take New York State Thruway to Exit 18 (New Paltz). In the center of town take Route 32 north for 8 miles; then take Route 213 west to the inns in the center of High Falls.

HOUSE ON THE HILL

Box 86, High Falls, NY 12440. 914-687-9627. *Innkeepers:* Shelly and Sharon Glassman. Open all year.

This "eyebrow" colonial with clapboard-over-stone construction was built in 1825; its gingerbreaded front porch and hand-forged iron fence were added in 1856. Giant locust trees flank the house, while maples line the drive and a grove of evergreens provides a tranquil setting to the grounds. The woodland behind the little pond on the hillside is home to many species of birds and wildflowers as well as a family of deer who are occasionally seen drinking at the water's edge.

The entranceway to the House on the Hill opens to a cheerful center hall. Here a staircase leads to a small sitting area on the landing and to the bedrooms beyond. Each room is named for its special feature: the Gray Room has muted gray wallpaper with sprays of mountain laurel blossoms; the Twin Room has matching iron bedsteads, each under one of the low "eyebrow" windows whose trim is punctuated with blue tones against the plain white–plastered walls. In the White Room a splash of color is added by the handsome star-pattern quilt draped over the spool bed. Wideboard pine floors throughout the inn are covered with rag rugs or, in some cases, Orientals. The theme of antique furnishings and handmade American quilts is continued in each of the inn's guest rooms.

Downstairs, the Keeping Room has its original fireplace with crane and irons. Here, eleven doors lead to various sections of the house. One leads to the glassed-in porch used for breakfasts in warm weather, another, to the country kitchen where guests can curl up in the sitting area and look out at the pond, woods, and old pink-brick smokehouse.

Guests are invited to join the Glassmans for wine and cheese by the fireside in cool weather or out on the front porch in summer. Any guests wishing a tour of the grounds and the nearby canal towpath are proudly escorted by the Glassman's young son Gregory and his entourage of family pets. The inn is within walking distance of two fine restaurants, one being the Depuy Canal House Tavern (which see).

High Falls is near year-round activities such as downhill and cross-country skiing at Hunter Mountain and Lake Mohonk. Swimming, boating, and fishing can be enjoyed at Roundout Creek and Falls. The area abounds with other recreational facilities as well as antique shops and museums.

Accommodations: 6 rooms, 1 with private bath. *Pets:* Not permitted. *Driving Instructions:* Take the New York State Thruway to exit 18. Take Route 299 west to Route 32. Drive north to Route 213 and take it west 3 miles to High Falls.

Hillsdale, New York

L'HOSTELLERIE BRESSANE

Corner of Routes 22 and 23, Hillsdale, New York. Mailing address: Box 387, Hillsdale, N.Y. 12529. 518-325-3412. *Innkeepers:* Jean and Madeleine Morel. Open all year except February and either March or April (call first).

Most gourmets know that out there somewhere, waiting for them, is a tiny, charming country inn where the food — French, of course — is absolute perfection. Well, search no more. Such a place does exist in the upstate New York farm town of Hillsdale near the Massachusetts border. L'Hostellerie Bressane is a wonderful little inn with two innkeepers, Chef Jean Morel and his wife, Madeleine. Jean Morel, named Master Chef of France by l'Association des maîtres cuisinier de France, serves only classical French cuisine and has been awarded four stars by just about everyone. This is one of the country's finest restaurants. Chef Morel comes from the French region of Bresse, was extensively schooled in France, and is a member of Cordons Bleus de Dijon, Vatel Club de N.Y., Société Culinaire Philanthropique, Cuisiniers de Paris, Maître Cusinier de France, and Académie Culinaire de France. He was the chef at New York's Chateaubriand and the Lafayette. Friends who knew of his dream of a small country place of his own called to tell him of this old brick inn in Hillsdale. He purchased it in 1971, and he and Madeleine completely restored and refurbished it with many of their heirlooms and antiques from France and the Netherlands.

The inn was built as a private home in 1783. It is constructed entirely of handmade bricks, and many of the windows are Palladian in design. The building has nine fireplaces, including one in each of the guest rooms and dining rooms, and the large chimneys for the fireplaces support each end of the house. Each of the four dining rooms is delightful in its own way.

And the food! More gastronomic fantasies are offered than we could possibly list here, but a hint of the pleasures follows. For starters, consider pâté de campagne à la façon du paysan bressan; coquilles Saint-Jacques aux champignons frais; and artichoke with foie gras and a sauce of black truffles. Seafood offerings include sole stuffed with fresh scallops, shad roe with sorrel sauce, and a special salad of lobster tails, avocado, goose liver, truffles, and watercress served with Boston lettuce. Among the many meat and poultry entrées are fresh pheasant with duck-liver sauce and wild rice, and veal kidney with a mustard cream sauce. Wines may be selected from one of the finest cellars in a country inn or, in fact, anywhere outside a large urban French restaurant. Here are many vintages and great wines.

The guest rooms are reminiscent of a country home in France or the Netherlands, with rough plastered walls, original old fireplaces (not in use), and huge old cupboards complete with the original hardware, which combine with the simple furnishings and pine-shaded windows to give an Old-World atmosphere. The two front rooms have views of the hills, and the rooms in the back have a peaceful diffused light from the tree-shaded windows. And, of course, just down the stairs, the food of Chef Jean Morel.

If you fall in love with the food, you can return for a four-day cooking school led by Chef Morel. Write for details.

Accommodations: 4 rooms with shared baths. *Pets:* Not permitted. *Driving Instructions:* From New York City, take the Taconic Parkway to Route 23 east. The inn is on the corner of Routes 23 and 22. From Boston or Lenox, take the Massachusetts Turnpike across the border to the Thruway spur. Take the first exit onto Route 22 south. Take Route 22 to the corner of Route 23 in Hillsdale.

Hunter, New York

HERITAGE INN

Main Street (Route 23A), Hunter, NY. Mailing address: Box 663, Hunter, NY 12442. 518-263-4333. Open all year; restaurant closed on Mondays.

The Heritage Inn is a large, sprawling, black-shuttered white farmhouse whose front porch curls around the jogs in the front of the building. The Heritage was one of the first buildings erected in Hunter. It was constructed by chair-factory owner Willis Baldwin, and an inscription in his own hand dated 1865 is still visible in the attic. A century ago, the hemlocks in this area were of immense proportions. Vertical planking the breadth of a man's arm can be seen in the inn, proof of the size of the virgin timber from which it was constructed.

As you enter the Heritage, you will be greeted by four dining rooms whose tables are set with white linens, crystal stemware, and fresh flowers. Stenciled Hitchcock chairs are the rule here and throughout the inn. There is a comfortable living room warmed by a wood-burning stove in the winter. Guest rooms at the Heritage feature antique beds (queen-sized canopy, cannon ball, brass, and Jenny Lind), pure-down comforters, and Colonial print wallpapers.

Nestled among the Catskills, the Heritage Inn is but 500 feet from the entrance to Hunter Ski Bowl. Schoharie Creek, one of the best fly-fishing spots in the state, is just across the street, and there are dozens of state-owned hiking trails within minutes. Hunter Mountain not only offers skiing but also has four important summer festivals — polka, Celtic, country-Western, and German. There are numerous fine antique and gift shops in the greater Hunter area.

Accommodations: 8 guest rooms, none with private bath, plus a cottage with 3 efficiencies, each with bath. *Pets:* Not permitted; kennels nearby. *Children:* "Mature" children only; inquire for definition. *Driving Instructions:* Take New York Thruway to Exit 20 at Saugerties and drive north on Routes 32 and 32A to Palenville. Then drive 12 miles west on Route 23A to Hunter and the inn.

Leonardsville, New York

HORNED DORSET INN

Main Street, Route 8, Leonardsville, NY 13364. 315-855-7898.
Open all year.

The Horned Dorset Inn is the result of the restoration of two adjacent
buildings: an Italianate villa that provides overnight accommodations; and a revitalized commercial building housing a highly
acclaimed French restaurant. The Italianate villa is actually the result
of a "modernization" in 1874 of an 1825 Federal-style home. As a
result, although most of the detailing is High Victorian, one can still
see the beautiful, perfectly preserved Federal circular cherry staircase
within the villa and the original wideboard pine floor in its library. In
the restoration Italian tiles from old designs were installed on the ves-

tibule floor, and authentic gas fixtures and globes were put in to light the 1870s portion of the house. Guest rooms are tucked into the sloping eaves above the bays and curves of the villa's original parlor, dining room, and vestibule.

The restaurant building was restored with the liberal use of period architectural elements in a successful attempt to create an atmosphere of times past. Hard yellow pine paneling, a balustraded dais, built-in bookcases, plastered walls, authentic gas fixtures, and an English Axminster carpet detail the main dining room. In the second dining room hand-stenciled and carved black walnut cornices and columns, a hand-wrought iron balustrade on marble steps, and a matching travertine mantelpiece are juxtaposed with large Palladian windows that look out to the garden and the villa beyond. Another room, with floor-to-ceiling birch paneling, is used for private dinner parties. A library for cocktails at the top of the stairs is also accented with black walnut woodwork. House specialties at the Horned Dorset are the chef's filet d'agneau, veal chasseur, saumon en croute, and sole bonne femme.

Accommodations: 2 rooms and 2 suites, all with private bath. *Pets:* Permitted. *Young children:* Not permitted. *Driving Instructions:* Take Route 8 south 4 miles from the New York State Thruway.

Millbrook, New York

ALTAMONT INN AND CONFERENCE CENTER

Route 343, Millbrook, NY 12545. 914-677-3161. *Innkeeper:* Donald B. Blackburn. Open most of the year.

Altamont, a rust-colored Georgian brick building on a hilltop, is surrounded by 100 acres of fields and woods. Its guest rooms are furnished rather formally in period pieces that complement the Georgian architecture. Four contain fireplaces, many have four-posters, Oriental rugs, and easy chairs.

The public rooms have Chippendale-style (and other) furnishings, more Oriental rugs, a staircase in the front hall, and French windows on the ground floor. The recreation room is well equipped. Bowling, croquet, and badminton are played on the lawn. An outdoor swimming pool, golf, and tennis are nearby. Breakfast is the only meal served, except to conventions and special parties.

Accommodations: 13 rooms, 6 with private bath. *Pets:* The inn prefers that guests do not bring pets, as it has a number of animals of its own. *Driving Instructions:* From west of Millbrook, take Route 44 east through the traffic light at Bennett College in Millbrook. From the light, take Route 343 east about 1½ miles to the inn (on the south side of Route 343). From east of Millbrook, take Route 22 to Dover Plains, then take Route 343 west to the inn's driveway. Do not turn on Altamont Road. The inn has a lighted sign at the gatehouse at the bottom of its driveway, which is ½ mile long.

THE KITTLE HOUSE

Route 117, Mount Kisco, New York. Mailing address: P.O. Box 448, Mount Kisco, NY 10549. 914-666-8044. *Innkeeper:* Edward Hawkins. Open all year.

The 190-year-old Kittle House has the distinction, we believe, of being the closest country inn to New York City. As such, it has enjoyed continued popularity as a corporate retreat during the week and a fast-getaway weekend spot for harried city dwellers. Much of the main floor at the Kittle House is devoted to food and drink, with a main dining room, the Carriage Room (for banquets), and the Tap Room. The latter has a large 150-year-old bar that was brought into this country by actress Fanny Brice for gangster Dutch Schultz during Prohibition. The bar, used in a speakeasy in those days, fell into disrepair before being bought twenty years ago and installed in the inn.

The table d'hôte menu at Kittle House offers a broad selection of starters, most of which are included in the basic meal price. Entrées include chicken, seafood, and several cuts of steak. Guest rooms are done in painted reproductions of period furniture, with modern amenities including wall-to-wall carpeting, air conditioning, color television, and room phones.

Kittle House is a good base for exploring the Rip Van Winkle countryside. Sleepy Hollow Restorations maintains Van Cortland Manor in Croton-on-Hudson (a restored late-eighteenth-century Dutch-English manor house), the Tarrytown mansion Lyndhurst, and Philipsburg Manor, also in Tarrytown and the site of a number of eighteenth-century crafts demonstrations. In a Mediterranean-style villa in Katonah, the Caramoor Center for Music and the Arts contains collected art covering more than nine centuries. In season, Caramoor also has concerts and children's-theater productions.

Accommodations: 15 rooms with private bath. *Pets:* Not permitted. *Driving Instructions:* Take Route 684 to the Mount Kisco exit for Route 172. Take Route 172 west to Route 117, turn south, and drive 1½ miles to the inn at the top of the hill.

MOHONK MOUNTAIN HOUSE

New Paltz, NY 12561. 914-255-1000 (New York City: 212-233-2244). *Innkeeper:* Frank Hamilton. Open all year.

There is nothing else like the Mohonk Mountain House. With 245 rooms and 151 fireplaces, one can tell at a glance that this is no secluded country inn. What it is, however, is an unforgettable experience in vacationing that is so unusual that we could not resist including it.

The Mohonk Mountain House began in 1869 when Albert and Alfred Smiley, twin brothers and Quaker schoolteachers, discovered the 280-acre parcel of land that included a ten-room tavern perched beside the crystal blue Lake Mohonk. They immediately purchased the property and set out to convert the tavern to a guest establishment that was more in keeping with their Quaker training. Drinking, dancing, smoking, and card playing were forbidden. The Smileys invited their friends to join them on a share-the-expenses basis. Without any advertising, the fame of the Smiley place grew. The brothers spent the period from 1870 to 1903 gradually expanding the buildings until today the hotel is one-eighth of a mile long and can accommodate five hundred guests.

Mohonk retains its nineteenth-century character, although some of its traditions have changed. There are still classical concerts, prayer services, and afternoon tea. There is no formal bar, but bottled liquor is available for purchase and consumption in private, and alcoholic beverages are available with the evening meal. Smoking is now permitted except in the dining room, parlor, and library. Carriage rides, once the only means of transportation to the hotel, are now offered for pleasure and are an excellent way of touring the grounds. And what grounds they are! With its thousands of acres of surrounding woodland, beautiful, award-winning gardens, miles of horse trails, and even a medieval-looking tower high above the lake, the resort is one of unparalleled beauty. Victorian splendor reigns here, perhaps best exemplified by the parlor. Designed by New York City architect James E. Ware at the turn of the century, its huge leaded-glass windows afford a spectacular view of the lake, the gardens, and the Skytop Tower. Velvet-covered sofas and chairs, an organ, a grand

piano, and fireplaces rest under the watchful eyes of portraits of the founding Smileys.

The Mohonk designs a special menu each day. Entrées might include fresh lobster Newburg, veal parmigiana, and roast loin of pork.

The Mohonk Mountain House is peaceful and inviting — one is apt to forget the size of the place in its atmosphere of attention to the needs of the guests. If you plan a visit, it is helpful to send for the current catalog of Mohonk events.

Accommodations: 295 rooms, 203 with private bath. (Some rooms have fireplaces.) *Pets:* Not permitted. *Driving Instructions:* Take exit 18 from the New York Thruway. Turn left on Route 299 and follow Main Street through New Paltz. Immediately after crossing the bridge, turn right (there is a "Mohonk" sign) and bear left following Mountain Rest Road (county Route 6) to the gate of the Mohonk Mountain House.

New York, New York

AMERICAN STANHOPE

995 Fifth Avenue, New York, NY 10028. 212-288-5800. *Innkeeper:* H. M. Singh Oberoi. Open all year.

As you step into the American Stanhope, you step into America's nineteenth century at its best. This small hotel of 160 rooms opposite the Metropolitan Museum is an ideal choice for guests who seek out the ambience of a European-style hotel with Upper East Side convenience. Mimi Russell, the hotel's owner and daughter of Lady Sarah Spencer-Churchill and *Vogue* publisher Edwin Russell, has filled the Stanhope with a superb collection of Empire and Victorian furniture and an extensive collection of nineteenth-century artwork.

Guest rooms blend Laura Ashley papers and fabrics with carefully chosen antiques and selected reproduction pieces. On the ground floor, guests may dine in either The Furnished Room, named for the O'Henry short story, or the Saratoga Room, where a full menu includes entrées such as sautéed calf's liver, roast Maryland chicken, Philadelphia mixed grill, and sautéed Idaho trout. In the summer, The Terrace offers sidewalk dining in the shadow of the Metropolitan. No shops, beauty salons, or other commercial distractions disturb the residential calm of the Stanhope. Parking is available beneath the museum, a distinct advantage in Manhattan. Free limosine service downtown is provided weekday mornings.

Accommodations: 160 rooms with private bath. *Driving Instructions:* The hotel is at Eighty-first Street and Fifth Avenue.

GARNET HILL LODGE

North River, NY 12856. 518-251-2821. *Innkeepers:* George and
Mary Heim. Open all year.

Garnet Hill was built in the 1930s to accommodate miners who
worked the nearby garnet mine. The lodge is an authentic split-log
"Adirondack lodge" of a type that is fast disappearing from this area.
Also on the property is the original mine owner's house which now
contains additional guest rooms used by the lodge.

The log lodge has a commanding view of 13th Lake and the surrounding countryside. The interior of the lodge is mostly finished
with exposed split-log walls, but some of the guest rooms have either
pine paneling or wallpaper. The main floor of the lodge has a large
general-purpose room dominated by a large garnet stone fireplace in
the center of the room with benches around it for the enjoyment of
winter fires. Also in this room is the dining area, with its pine trestle
tables, a card-playing area, and regular and bumper pool tables.

The lodge is filled with the smell of freshly baking bread, one of
the Heims' specialties. The lodge has a small menu, augmented by
several daily specials. Although the menu changes somewhat each
week, a typical selection might include roast beef, turkey, lasagna, or
gnocchi. Several vegetables and salads are available.

Typical guest rooms sleep up to four persons—in a double bed
(many are heavy brass) plus a set of bunk beds. Some of the rooms
have modern private baths, and most have a homey look with
"Grandma Moses" curtains, desks, and chairs.

Garnet Hill has a complete ski-touring center, with instruction,
sales and rentals, and 20 miles of groomed trails. These trails make for
excellent hiking in the summer; a hike to the abandoned garnet mine
to hunt for garnets and enjoy the view of the lake is particularly
popular. Guests in the summer also enjoy swimming, sailing, and
canoeing on the lake.

Accommodations: 25 rooms, 15 with private bath. *Pets:* Not permitted. *Driving Instructions:* From the information center at the
intersection of Routes 28 and 8, take Route 28 north to the intersection of Routes 28 and 28N. Continue 5.4 miles north on Route 28
and then turn left at 13th Lake Road at the Towne Grocery. Take this
road 5 miles to the lodge.

Portageville, New York

GENESEE FALLS INN AND MOTEL

Route 436, Portageville, NY 14536. 716-493-2484. *Innkeepers:*
Lea and Ed Brosche. Open all year except January and December.
The innkeeping tradition on lot 98 at the corner of Main and Hamilton goes back to 1824, when a simple mill tavern was constructed on
the site to serve the traveler and the local men working the logging
camps. That building and the one built to replace it were both destroyed by fire. However, the present structure, built of brick in 1870
by innkeeper Joseph Ingham, has survived practically unchanged

since that date. The three-story inn was always a popular spot on the Genesee River. The rooms were typical of the period — comfortable but not fancy. Dances were frequently held on Saturday night in the third-floor ballroom, where the great boxer John L. Sullivan also gave several exhibitions. Over the years the inn passed through several owners. Modernization came slowly but surely — running water was brought to each floor in 1913 and to every room in 1944. The hotel was one of few that survived Prohibition without many scars, probably because the region, with its abundance of scenery, remained an attraction, to say nothing of a reliable supply of whiskey cleverly buried in the inn's basement coal bin. Many original architectural components are still in place, including the original pressed-tin ceiling in the lobby and hall. The old wooden floor had to be replaced in 1915 by tile floors, the wood having been destroyed by the calks (spiked plates) on loggers' shoes.

The inn's lobby and dining room have the original tall hexagonal windows. There is a profusion of colored glassware and antiques, as well as antique china cabinets, period furniture, and a collection of early items of decorative art, including a gold-framed mirror that once belonged to Vice-President Schuyler Colfax, who served under Ulysses S. Grant. The mirror hangs in the formal dining room with its ceramic tile floor, Hepplewhite buffet, and an exposed-beam ceiling. The dining room offers a selection of traditional American fare.

Guest rooms at the inn are furnished with period furniture set against old-fashioned wallpapers. One room has an antique brass bed while others have four-poster twin or double beds. Most have early marble-topped tables. Guests who prefer early-inn furnishings should ask for one of the period rooms, because the inn also offers five motel-type rooms in a recent addition furnished with new pieces. The Genesee Falls Inn is a comfortable place where guests feel at home, playing cards, getting together in the taproom, or enjoying the scenery of nearby Letchworth State Park.

Accommodations: 12 rooms, 10 with private bath. *Pets:* Not permitted. *Driving Instructions:* Portageville is south of Warsaw, New York, on Route 436E.

INN AT QUOGUE

Quogue Street, Quogue, NY 11959. 516-653-6560. *Innkeeper:* Susan McAllister. Open mid-May to mid-September.

In the evening the crisp white exterior of the Inn at Quogue is gently illuminated by lights tucked among the tall trees surrounding the nearly two-hundred-year-old building. For many years the inn was known as Hallock House, one of several boarding houses in this quiet seaside village in the Hamptons. Susan McAllister purchased the house and created a casual country inn with a restaurant noted for its understated elegance and fine food.

On the first floor are the main dining room, a fireplace bar, and two attractive suites. Bentwood chairs surround tables whose glass tops protect floral-print cloths. Chef Starr Boggs has gained local renown for his treatment of fish fresh from Long Island's waters. In addition to flounder, scallops, striped bass, and bluefish, Mr. Boggs frequently serves grilled mako shark and other less frequently encountered denizens of the cold waters off Montauk Point. Duckling, veal, and steak dishes round out his repertoire.

Guest rooms at the inn are simply decorated using antique bedsteads accented by Victorian bric-a-brac and period furniture. In cooler months there is usually a fire in the bar's fireplace. Overstuffed sofas surround the hearth, encouraging guests to linger and enjoy the live music presented several days each week.

Accommodations: 14 rooms, 11 with private bath. *Pets:* Not permitted. *Children:* Not encouraged. *Driving Instructions:* From the west, take exit 63 off the Long Island Expressway (Route 495). Drive south to Route 27A, turn east, and drive to Jessup Avenue. Turn south and drive to the center of town.

BEEKMAN ARMS

Route 9, Rhinebeck, NY 12572. 914-876-7077. *Innkeeper:* Earl Bebo. Open all year.

The Beekman Arms is generaly considered to be the oldest hotel in the country. It has, by any measure, a most illustrious history, having entertained several presidents including George Washington and both Roosevelts. Other notables who have been guests at this famous hostelry include Aaron Burr, the Marquis de Lafayette, Horace Greeley, and William Jennings Bryan, to name but a few. The inn was built in sections, the earliest dating from 1700. The tiny original two-room stone building erected that year offered only meager comfort for weary travelers and was finally, in 1766, replaced by the first of the buildings that survive today.

The new inn was built by Arent Traphagen and was a fortress-like structure with a full second story and stone walls 2 and 3 feet thick. Its 8 by 12-inch oak beams and 2-inch-thick plank floors made this the most secure building in the area. Over the ensuing years the building has been enlarged and has mellowed. It is reassuring to note, however, that the entire inn reflects the feeling of colonial traditions and workmanship. In even the most recent addition, old red brick and carefully selected wide boards and heavy beams have been used to carry out this theme. Visitors can find a multitude of antique furnishings throughout. The paneled walls are hung with examples of the inn's colonial heritage—muskets, sabers, powder horns, maps, deeds, pistols, lithographs, and corncob pipes.

The Tap Room at the inn is a lovely old paneled room with dark heavy beams, a natural wood floor, and a large, attractive bar. Dinner at the Beekman Arms may be selected from an à la carte menu that lists ten appetizers and nineteen entrées. Choices range from their deservedly famous roast prime ribs of beef to chops, seafood, and poultry dishes that include a number of interesting special selections. Among these is eggplant di Carnevalle (layered eggplant with chopped spinach and Italian cheeses), breast of chicken Anthony, and shrimp tempura served with an Oriental dipping sauce. There is an extensive luncheon menu that includes crêpes, quiche, omelets, baked scallops,

and the same eggplant dish served at dinner, as well as a number of sandwiches. Breakfast is not served, except for Sunday Brunch.

Accommodations: 18 rooms with private bath. *Driving Instructions:* The inn is in the center of Rhinebeck on Route 9.

WINTER CLOVE INN

Winter Clove Road, Round Top, New York. *Mailing address:* Box 67, Round Top, NY 12473. 518-622-3267. *Innkeeper:* Edward Whitcomb. Open all year.

Winter Clove is a four-story mansard-roofed inn built in 1860, with additions by the current innkeeper's grandfather in the 1870s. In 1962 two motel units were constructed on the property, as well as a large indoor swimming pool and bowling lanes. These more recent additions have allowed Winter Clove to become a full-scale resort, but it still retains its historical perspective through its restored guest rooms in the original inn.

Winter Clove is on 400 acres, of which approximately 25 are landscaped. A broad, delicately arched porch runs the entire length of the inn building, which contains thirty-five of the guest rooms, all comfortably furnished and many with wideboard pine floors, braided rugs, and four-poster beds. The common areas are carpeted and have upholstered "colonial" furniture drawn up to stone fireplaces, or more modern lounge furniture in the glass-enclosed solarium and greenhouse.

Winter Clove is an American Plan resort with full breakfasts, hot or cold luncheons, and complete four-course dinners included in the room rates. Luncheon might include such dishes as meatloaf with mushroom gravy, or sliced turkey; dinner could offer a choice of roast meats with all the fixings. The inn's recreational facilities include a heated indoor pool, an outdoor pool, a nine-hole golf course, tennis, bowling, hiking, and cross-country skiing.

Winter Clove has been in the same family for five generations. Even today, desserts are made by the innkeeper's mother or cousin, and other family members are involved in the operation of Winter Clove on a daily basis.

Accommodations: 50 rooms, 48 with private bath, 15 in two motel units. *Pets:* Not permitted. *Driving Instructions:* From Catskill, take Route 23 west to Cairo. Turn at the blinker light and drive uphill to Round Top. From there, follow the signs to Winter Clove.

Saranac Lake, New York

THE POINT

Star Route, Saranac Lake, NY 12983. 518-891-5674. *Innkeeper:* Edward Carter. Open all year except April.

A stay at The Point is a luxurious experience. It was formerly one of the last of the grand old private camps that used to dot the shores of Upper Saranac Lake. The spot had been chosen for its natural beauty and solitude and had served as the private retreat of the Rockefeller family and the scene of many gatherings of celebrities such as statesmen, prominent society people, and royalty.

The Point was built here in the 1930s as an Adirondack lodge using peeled pine and cedar logs. Several buildings make up the compound.

The Long House contains the Great Hall, an architectural triumph with timber ceilings, overstuffed furniture, trophy skins, and massive twin fireplaces facing each other across the baronial expanse of the room. The terrace offers excellent vistas of the lake, which provides all manner of aquatic attractions in summer and which in winter is open to skaters and to cross-country skiers, who enjoy exploring more than 500 miles of trails, both on and off the lake. The Boathouse is the center of much of the activity at The Point. A flotilla of rowboats, canoes, and speedboats is kept here, including a silver speedboat that looks as if it had just come from a James Bond movie set. In warm weather a barge sets off from here for evening cocktail cruises. After dinner the Boathouse's game room becomes a ballroom, complete with a veranda. In winter there are fires in the hearth on the upper deck, and one can sip hot drinks and watch skaters on the illuminated rink below.

Each bedroom at The Point has its own special feature. Most have overhead paddle fans, cathedral ceilings, and stone fireplaces with stacks and stacks of wood. The innkeeper provides extra touches such as baskets of fruit and wine daily, as well as bouquets of fresh flowers. One room, Weatherwatch, has a private terrace overlooking the lake. Mohawk is an enormous master bedroom that opens into the library.

Meals are imaginatively presented at various spots around the compound. Generous country breakfasts are served in the sunny morning room, and lunches are sometimes cooked over a pinecone fire at the lake's edge. Evenings find guests gathered for cocktails and then dinner, which is usually served in Reindeer Hall. Typical selections include roasts, freshly baked breads and pastries, and fresh vegetables. Imported wines are available as well. When the weather is right, dinner may be served aboard one of the lodge's boats.

Accommodations: 8 rooms with private bath. *Children:* Not permitted. *Driving Instructions:* The lodge is about 6 hours north of New York City. Call or write the lodge for detailed driving instructions.

Saratoga Springs, New York

ADELPHI HOTEL

365 Broadway, Saratoga Springs, NY 12866. 518-587-4688. *Innkeepers:* Gregg Siefker and Sheila Parkert. Open May through October.

The Adelphi is one of the original High Victorian hotels that once graced Broadway in the center of the "Queen of the Spas," Saratoga, New York. Built in 1877, this small but grand hotel is an elegant building of Italianate design. A spectacular piazza with slender columns rising three stories to elaborate Victorian fretwork is the focal point of the building. Inside, an open stairwell climbs four stories past rooms and hallways, both high-ceilinged and appropriately wallpapered. Every room has undergone meticulous restoration. Most of the spacious guest rooms feature Victorian decor, but a few reflect the 1920s, when the hotel underwent some major renovations. There are lofty ceilings and windows framed with ornate Victorian woodwork. The rooms are handsomely decorated, and all have air conditioning and telephones. There are a few suites with small sitting rooms.

The public rooms are equally elegant. Breakfasts are offered in the High Victorian Parlor or on the Grand Piazza. There are also a Tea Room, a Victorian Bar, a Courtyard Café, and a Supper Club housed in the grand scarlet-and-gold ballroom. Each offers meals of varying substance from light teas with French pastries and other confections to full-course dinners consiting of French or international dishes. Some unusual dishes range from mosaic of veal, which is leg of veal stuffed with cheese and prosciutto, through salami-and-herb omelets, to baked goat cheese and prosciutto. Among the house specialties are soft-shell crabs with mustard hollandaise sauce, smoked chicken breast, and filet mignon served with Pinot Noir wine sauce and béarnaise sauce.

In addition to the famed mineral spa and eclectic Victorian architecture of Saratoga Springs, there are several seasonal attractions nearby, including the Saratoga Race Track, the oldest in the nation.

Accommodations: 17 rooms with private bath. *Pets:* Not permitted. *Driving Instructions:* The hotel is in the center of the historic district of Saratoga Springs.

AUBERGE DES QUATRE SAISONS

Route 42, Shandaken, NY 12480. 914-668-2223. *Innkeepers:* Annie and Dadou Labielle. Open weekends in winter and daily in summer.

The Auberge des Quatre Saisons has grown up around an 1870 building that still houses its restaurant and a number of inn-style rooms. It has a wide, modern redwood deck used for summer dining and relaxation. The furnishings here are country comfortable, and for those who like more modern accommodations there is a separate chalet-style motel building. In the latter, all rooms have private baths, as do some of the main inn rooms. On the grounds are tennis, a swimming pool, volleyball, boccie, table tennis, badminton, and croquet as well as the other amenities of a Catskills vacation.

But it is for the food that tourists flock to the Labielles' doorstep. Here amid the babbling trout streams and surrounding mountains is a truly fine French restaurant looked after by a master chef, Edouard Labielle. Perhaps the high point of a meal here is the locally caught trout, freshly cleaned and sautéed and served with parsley and garlic or with capers. Often the trout arrive *à table* as beautifully decorated as any you might receive in a fine urban French restaurant. Other specialties of the house include a platter of charcuteries, escargots, and terrine of pork among the well-prepared starters and duckling à l'orange and pot-au-feu of chicken and beef as entrées. The prix fixe dinner is a four-course sampler of the best of French country cooking. Breakfast is also served to both guests and the public, but lunch is not available.

Accommodations: 36 rooms, 17 with private bath. *Driving Instructions:* Take the New York Thruway to Exit 19 at Kingston. Take Route 28 west about 30 miles to Route 42. The inn is a mile north of Route 28.

Shelter Island, New York

CHEQUIT INN

23 Grand Avenue (Route 114), Shelter Island, NY 11965. Off-season mailing address: Route 1, Rogers, TX 76569. 516-749-0018. *Innkeeper:* Phillip Franzoni. Open May 1 through September (or until it gets cold).

The Chequit Inn, the *grande dame* of Shelter Island Heights, is on an island hillside amid a group of Victorian gingerbreads. The sprawling seaside inn comes straight out of the nineteenth century with hardly a gray hair or stick of furniture out of place. Its earliest section was built sometime around the 1860s as a Grange Hall. It was first licensed as an inn in 1871 and was known simply as "The Restaurant." The Restaurant served the many summer houses on the island that were built without kitchens (no one wanted to run a hot coal stove in the middle of summer). One of innkeeper Phil Franzoni's oldest childhood memories is of rising at the crack of dawn to fire up the coal stove for guests' breakfasts.

Phil's father and mother bought the inn in 1944 from people with the unfortunate name of Crooks, who had operated the place since the Roaring Twenties. The inn moved from innkeeper to innkeeper with most of her furnishings intact. The Franzonis have added many unusual pieces to the collections of spindle beds, ornate walnut and oak furniture, and white antique wicker that has been here since the nineteenth century. The lobby-lounge is lit by large brass chandeliers from the historic Old Montauk Yacht Club. Old cobbler's benches are placed in front of wicker sofas and elaborately scrolled wicker rockers. In the dining room is a mantelpiece from the New York apartment of William Randolph Hearst. To pay his bar tab, a local artist painted the mantel in color and added a spider web to the boarded-up hearth. Oil paintings grace the walls throughout the inn. The lounge, halls, and rooms are decorated with many antique Austrian mirrors and prints. In the cavernous bar downstairs the walls and beams are painted with humorous and attractive scenes.

The Chequit is a white clapboard structure surrounded by porches, terraces, and blue hydrangeas. It is on the hill just a short walk from the little town and marina on Dering Harbor and the North Ferry to Greenport. The lounge is a large room with a working fireplace, rosebud wallpaper, old prints, mirrors, and antiques. Drapes hang from the sturdy brass curtain rods. The dining room features traditional seaside cuisine with a menu that changes daily. Fresh fish and clam chowder, the specialties, are almost always offered along with a choice of at least five other entrées such as duck, roast pork, or veal. Local diners know that certain dishes regularly appear on appointed days of the week: Thursday, for example, is always corned beef and cabbage day.

It is difficult to pick a favorite guest room. Those in the annex across the way are the most in demand because they are larger and perhaps a little fancier. The main hotel features smaller rooms on its second and third floors. Rooms in both the annex and the inn are furnished with old-fashioned pieces complemented by the print wallpapers and white curtains. There are a wide variety of marble-tops, ornate walnut beds, spindle and spool beds, and general Victoriana. Phil Franzoni loves to refer to the furniture as "that old stuff," fully aware of the pleasant atmosphere it creates. As he says, "It's nostalgia—wake up and you're at Grandma's."

If the inn is full, as it frequently is in the peak summer months, ask Phil about rooms in his Shelter Harbor House nearby, which is open all year. It is a rambling Victorian building with a restaurant, very popular pub, and rooms in the process of being restored.

Accommodations: 44 rooms with private bath. *Pets:* Not permitted. *Driving Instructions:* Take Route 114 from either ferry to the center of the island; the inn is right on the route.

Skaneateles, New York

THE SHERWOOD INN

26 West Genesee St., Skaneateles, NY 13152. 315-685-3405.
Innkeeper: William B. Eberhardt. Open all year.

Isaac Sherwood was a man of large proportions both in body and in business. Weighing more than 300 pounds, he was the proprietor of a successful stagecoach enterprise. In 1807 he decided that it was time for him to build a proper headquarters for his expanding business, so he had a tavern built that could provide his office space as well. The tavern changed hands a number of times in the next few years, and in the mid-1860s the building was expanded considerably by one John Packwood, a successful carriage builder. At that time, a third floor, an east and a west wing, and a balcony were added. Although the inn was to pass through a number of hands over the next century, it was generally well maintained and its reputation prospered. The Sherwood Inn, recently fully overhauled and redecorated by the present innkeeper, is a lakefront hotel with natural wood floors and an abundance of antiques in all the rooms. Each guest room has an excellent view of Skaneateles Lake.

The restaurant at the Sherwood serves American food. Both lunch and dinner are available to guests and the public.

Accommodations: 13 rooms with private bath. *Pets:* Permitted, but only with advance notice. *Driving Instructions:* The inn is in the center of Skaneateles and may be reached by taking Route 20.

THE VILLAGE LATCH

101 Hill Street, Southampton, NY 11968. 516-283-2160. *Innkeepers:* Marta Byer-White and Martin White. Open May through November.

The Village Latch is set back on spacious, tree-shaped lawns behind high privet hedges. The inn is a handsome white clapboard estate house, once the annex to the old Irving Hotel, Southampton's oldest and poshest hostelry. The Irving's era of impeccable service, large black limousines, service bells, and servants everywhere is gone, as is the old Irving itself. The Latch is very much here. The inn is a quiet, private place appealing to young couples and single guests. Both innkeepers, Marta and Martin, have spent many hours restoring this old beauty to its former elegance. When the Irving closed, the annex was abandoned and stood empty for several years. Marta, Martin, and a team of carpenters and painters scraped, painted, and repaired until the place shone. The building retains its original floor-to-ceiling windows, wide French doors everywhere, old lighting fixtures, and paneled white wainscoting. The center of the inn is a large, sunny salon with a working fireplace and inviting groupings of comfortable couches and chairs. There are plants everywhere, including tall ficus and unusual pines in the salon-lounge and the sun parlor.

Recently the innkeepers moved four historic buildings onto 3 secluded acres behind the main inn, increasing the number of guest rooms and creating the atmosphere of a small resort-inn. One of these buildings has a country kitchen complete with a Garland range. Another, the Potting Shed, has a spacious living room, which is often used for small groups of businessmen who have sought out the Village Latch for a rural corporate retreat. But the outstanding addition is the all-glass conservatory, which now houses a hot-tub surrounded by comfortable lounge furniture.

All the rooms at the Village Latch, both in the main inn and in the recently transplanted buildings are filled with a comfortable clutter of antiques and near antiques. Marta, a fanatical collector of antiques of all sizes, shapes, periods, and flavors, is in addition a theatrical director and producer. She has furnished the inn with soft couches, soft rugs, and all sorts of furnishings gleaned almost daily from the posh auctions and yard sales one is apt to encounter in the Hamptons. Off the spacious lounge is the television room, containing the only set in the inn, along with a working fireplace and more antiques — cupboards and hutches full of them.

Perhaps the most fun of this place is the exploration and discovery of all the tiny nooks. Guests will find cupboards full of old baskets, a tiny wicker doll carriage with a funny old plant in it, a marble shelf with a crackly old doll perched on it, or a bust of a lovely maiden peering down from a hidden corner. The sun parlor is in a flanking wing of the inn. In it guests can relax amid many unusual plants, old advertising arts, lots of quilts and pillows, and an old iron bed *cum* couch. On the grounds is a tennis court, and within walking distance are the fashionable boutiques of Southampton's Jobs Lane and many of the village's finest restaurants.

Accommodations: 37 rooms, most with private baths. *Pets and Children:* Not permitted. *Driving Instructions:* Long Island Expressway (Route 495) to Exit 70. Take a right turn at the exit and go south to Route 27. Take Route 27 east to Southampton. Hill Street is an extension of Job's Lane, and the inn is next to the Southampton Inn.

Stephentown, New York

MILLHOF INN

Route 43, Stephentown, New York. *Mailing address:* Box 79, Hancock, MA 01237. 518-733-5606. *Innkeepers:* Frank Tallet and Ronnie Tallet. Open late May through March.

Millhof was built in 1935 as a sawmill and not converted to an inn until a decade ago or more. Appropriately, rough-sawn paneling and exposed beams play an important part in Millhof's decor. The building is reminiscent of a Swiss chalet, which contributes to the feeling that one is visiting a European *auberge* rather than an American inn in the New York Berkshires. Antique furnishings are the rule in the twin- and double-bedded rooms and suites, and a common room provides a gathering place with games and pleasant music; in season, an open fire there adds to a mellow feeling. Each guest room has private bath, individual heat control, and air conditioning. The nicely landscaped grounds include a kidney-shaped swimming pool bordered by a stone wall.

Millhof provides a good base for the exploration of the nearby Hancock Shaker Village. Be sure to see the Great Shaker Barn, the largest stone barn in the United States. Also nearby are Tanglewood, the Williamstown Theatre Festival, Clark Art Institute, Bennington Museum, and skiing at Jiminy Peak and Brodie Mountain.

Accommodations: 10 rooms with private bath. *Pets:* Not permitted. *Children:* Under twelve not permitted. *Driving Instructions:* Take Route 22 to Route 43. Turn east and go 1¼ miles to the inn.

THREE VILLAGE INN

150 Main Street, Stony Brook, NY 11790. 516-751-0555. *Innkeepers:* Nelson, Monda, and Whitney Roberts. Open all year except Christmas.

In the eighteenth century the Three Village Inn was the home of shipbuilder Jonas Smith. It still stands in one of Long Island's best-restored historic towns, Stony Brook, near the town marina and harbor just off the Sound. The inn is surrounded by ivy-covered pathways, flowering bushes, and shade trees, and in spring the place is brightened by a yellow forsythia in bloom on the hill. The inn is a white clapboard structure with unusual shuttered windows across the front. They reach to the floor and each has a single wide green shutter that is swung aside. The central chimney is typical of the mid-eighteenth century and services the three fireplaces in what had been the parlor, "settin' room," and cooking area. Today, these fireplaces and two more in The Sandbar pub are kept alight on chilly evenings.

As guests enter the inn they are immediately confronted by the sea captain's old staircase. Off to one side is the lobby where costumed staff members greet them. To the other side of the staircase is the parlor, with low, dark beams, a brick hearth, and old panels of deep-colored pine.

The Sandbar, the most informal of the dining rooms, has a long row of windows framing panes of thick bull's-eye glass. Brick hearths at either end and a dark wood bar work with the low rough-plastered ceilings and exposed heavy beams to create a feeling of colonial days. Antique sideboards and cupboards decorate the rooms, and lighted hutches display fine collections of antique china and Wedgwood.

The cuisine features a selection of early-American dishes. Among its specialties are clam pies, oysters and clams served in a variety of styles, and plenty of "fresh from the sea" fish entrées. In addition there are roasts, steaks, Long Island duck, and a chicken pie specialty.

Several small, old-fashioned guest rooms are upstairs in the inn, and many larger and more modern rooms are in little cottages behind it on the hill overlooking the harbor. The most requested room has a seaside view and a fireplace stocked with plenty of firewood. All rooms are decorated with a blend of period antiques and reproduction

furnishings. The innkeepers have provided easy-access lodgings and a ramp into the inn for handicapped guests.

Accommodations: 28 rooms in cottages or in the inn, with private bath. *Pets:* Not permitted. *Driving Instructions:* From New York City, take the Long Island Expressway–Route 495 to exit 62 and proceed north on Nichols Road to Route 25A. Turn left at the stoplight, go to the next stoplight, then turn right onto Main Street and continue to the "3VI."

Trumansburg, New York

TAUGHANNOCK FARMS INN

Route 89 at Taughannock Falls State Park, Trumansburg, NY 14886. 607-387-7711. *Innkeepers:* Nancy and C. Keith le Grand. Open April 1 to Thanksgiving.

A Mr. John Jones of Philadelphia came to the Finger Lakes region of New York in 1872 and, amid spectacular scenery overlooking Cayuga

Lake, built his elegant Victorian mansion. A stay here at Taughannock Farms is much like a trip back to Mr. Jones's time. The le Grands are the third generation to operate the old inn. It is a very close-knit family operation; most of the waitresses have been with the family for fifteen to twenty-five years.

The Taughannock Farms Inn, at the mouth of the Taughannock Gorge, offers guest rooms with the same fine Victorian furnishings as Mr. Jones's guests enjoyed back in the late nineteenth century. Upstairs are several parlor-sitting rooms for guests to relax and visit in. The cocktail lounge is quite popular and features marble-top tables with elaborately inlaid and carved wood bases and matching chests. The inn has four dining rooms, some with views of the lake. The rooms are most gracious and serve dinners to guests and the public.

The menu has fifteen entrées including many roasts: prime ribs, duckling, Cornish game hens, and lamb. Meals are quite a bargain; each of the entrées is accompanied by an appetizer, three vegetables, assorted homemade relishes, hot, freshly baked rolls, orange date bread, salad, a beverage, and dessert. Desserts are great fun to choose —there is a vast array of home-baked pies, pastries, and sundaes.

The inn may be reached for dinner by means of the "Cayuga Queen," a seasonal tour boat which makes daily dinner runs from the Allan H. Treman Marina to the inn and back. Reservations advised.

Accommodations: 4 rooms, 1 with private bath. *Pets:* Not permitted. *Driving Instructions:* Eight miles north of Ithaca on Route 89, the inn is forty minutes south of the New York Thruway's exit 41.

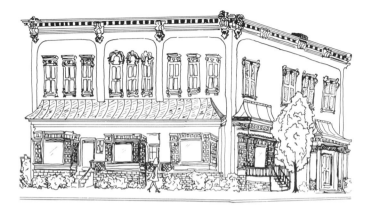

Westport, New York

THE INN ON THE LIBRARY LAWN

1 Washington Street, Westport, NY. Mailing address: Box 381, Westport, NY 12993. 518-962-8666. *Innkeepers:* Scott and Doreen Willard. Open all year but restaurant is closed in April.

The Inn on the Library Lawn has crisp, clean lines; sparkling, multipaned windows; and manicured, landscaped grounds. In addition to being well cared for, it has the bonus of being situated in one of the loveliest spots in New York's north country, overlooking historic Lake Champlain and the distant Green Mountains of Vermont. Stretching for miles to the west of the inn is the immense and wild Adirondack Park with its high mountain peaks.

This classic clapboard inn with its intricate detailing was built in the early 1900s as an annex for the old Westport Inn, which has since gone the way of many of the grand hotels of the steamship era that once lined the shores of the Great Lakes. The inn was repiped, replumbed, rewired, and generally redone with a capital *R*. Inside, the walls were papered with old-fashioned prints above natural wood wainscoting. Each of the guest rooms is an attractive blend of old and new. They have rocking chairs and mirror-topped bureaus shown to their best advantage against the striped print wallpapers. Three rooms overlook the lake and the sweep of lawn running down to the inn's beach, while another, smaller room looks out into the cedar trees. In the Common Room, upstairs, overnight guests can relax and visit with other guests or curl up with a book. The inn's solitary television set resides in this room, which is also decorated with antiques.

Just off the lobby a collection of antique chairs and an old carriage bench is grouped around a working fireplace. The wainscoted dining room overlooks the lake and the mountains beyond. Its menu includes omelets, fish, and salads at lunch. At dinner the inn offers fresh fish of the day, homemade soups, duck and veal dishes, and crepes.

The inn, an all-season resort, offers 18 miles of groomed cross-country ski trails serviced by its own ski-touring center. There are a heated pool and an eighteen-hole golf course, as well as two tennis courts. All common water sports are available at the lakefront.

Accommodations: 11 rooms, 10 with private bath; 5 cottages. *Pets:* Not permitted. *Driving Instructions:* Take Route I-87 to Route 9N to Westport.

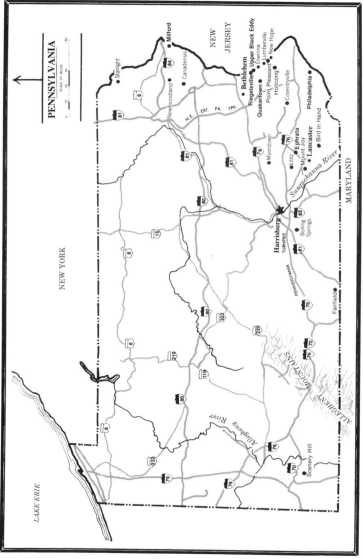

Pennsylvania

Bethlehem, Pennsylvania

THE HOTEL BETHLEHEM

437 Main Street, Bethlehem, PA 18018. 215-867-3711. *Innkeeper:* Elizabeth Emslander. Open all year.

The first house in Bethlehem was built on the exact site of the Hotel Bethlehem in 1745. In time, a total of three hotels would succeed each other in the same spot, the Hotel Bethlehem, built in 1921, being the last in the chain. One of the reasons for the popularity of this site for overnight accommodations was that its location could serve two local stagecoach roads. Indeed, the hotel's driveway is the Old York Road, and nearby is the Old Ohio Road, another ancient stagecoach run. The construction of the hotel in 1921 was brought about by an unusual piece of financing hardly possible in this day and age. The citizens of Bethlehem felt, as did many others in neighboring cities, that if Bethlehem was to be a first-class city it would have to have a first-class hotel. Thus the townspeople issued a public stock offering and used the proceeds from the common and preferred stock sold to construct the finest hotel in the area.

The Hotel Bethlehem survives as a fine monument to first-class travel of another era. Do not let the unpretentious exterior put you off. Inside, this small hotel has made into its trademark a variety of personal services that you are unlikely to find elsewhere. Among its many courtesies are free 24-hour limousine service, turn-down service in all guest rooms, custom-made towels that are 3 by 6 feet, four individual and different types of soap in every room, a shoe horn by each bed, sewing kits, a small library of books and current magazines in each room, and much more. You will find fresh flowers in the elevator foyers as well as on the breakfast table (long-stemmed red roses are a tradition). There are king-size or queen-size beds in most rooms, and some bathrooms have a sunken tub (at least one has room enough for two, a romantic notion). Some guest rooms even have 1 ½ baths. For guests who return more than five times, a guest history is started. This includes the hobbies, favorite colors, food preferences, birthday, and special interests of the guest. Then on return visits you might find a special magazine of interest to you waiting in your room or a birthday cake delivered to your table unannounced on your birthday. Clearly, all of this sets the Bethlehem apart from almost any other hotel of its size.

Sadly, the distinguished French restaurant that gave the Bethlehem Hotel some of its more recent fame has closed. In its place, there is a perfectly satisfactory though far less ornate restaurant in the Pioneer Room that serves steaks, chicken Kiev, veal Cordon Bleu, stuffed shrimp, and the like. If you feel like being pampered while visiting this city of contrasts, the Hotel Bethlehem is your best bet.

Accommodations: 125 rooms with private bath. *Driving Instructions:* The inn is on Main Street in Bethlehem.

Bird in Hand, Pennsylvania

GREYSTONE MOTOR LODGE

2658 Old Philadelphia Pike, Bird in Hand, Pennsylvania. Mailing address: P.O. Box 270, Bird in Hand, PA 17505. 717-393-4233. *Innkeepers:* Jim and Phyllis Reed. Open all year.

In 1883, the present Greystone Motor Lodge was constructed from a farmhouse that had stood on the site since the middle of the century. In building the Greystone, its owners set out to re-create a typical French Second Empire Victorian mansion. Its stately columns, segmented arches, high Victorian windows, and imposing bay window are typical of the post–Civil War period, when American architects mixed Italianate and mansarded styles.

Guest rooms at Greystone are in both the mansion and its carriage house. Several of the rooms have features such as stained-glass windows, cut-crystal doors, and antique furnishings. The mansion's lobby is typically Victorian, with beveled glass doors, antique lighting fixtures, and molded plaster ceiling and wall decorations. Situated on 2 acres of grounds, the Greystone offers air conditioning and television, private baths, and full kitchens in some suites of rooms. Because of the variety of accommodations at Greystone, we suggest asking for details about the specific room in which you will be staying.

Accommodations: 10 rooms and suites, all with private bath. *Pets:* Not permitted. *Driving Instructions:* The inn is on the south side of Route 340, one block west of the railroad overpass in Bird in Hand.

Boiling Springs, Pennsylvania

ALLENBERRY RESORT INN AND PLAYHOUSE

Boiling Springs, PA 17007. 717-258-3211. *Innkeeper:* The Heinze family. Open April through October.

We hasten to mention that Allenberry is a large resort with tennis courts, swimming pools, conference centers, and banquet halls. Were this the full story at Allenberry, it would not have been included in these pages. On the other hand, the resort has grown up around two very old, typical Pennsylvania buildings, and these retain their early character in a way that may well attract an inn lover who is eager to enjoy the kind of pampering that only a full-service resort can be expected to offer.

The original land grants for the property came from William Penn in 1865. The property was developed as a genteel country estate in the late eighteenth and early nineteenth centuries. A succession of owners, including cousins of Davy Crockett, maintained the property until 1944 when the Heinze family purchased it and began the current development as a resort.

The two oldest buildings are Fairfield Hall (1785), now used as the main dining room, offices, lounge, and gift shop, and Stone Lodge (1814). The latter offers the most innlike atmosphere with its fifteen "colonial" guest rooms. The lower level of this expansive stone structure contains a gourmet restaurant and the main cocktail lounge, which often has live entertainment. In addition to the accommodations in the Stone Lodge, there are thirty-two motel rooms in the recently constructed Meadow Lodge, as well as log-cabin cottages of various sizes set in the woods, all with housekeeping facilities.

Much of the focus of the Allenberry Resort is on its Allenberry Playhouse, which features the "best of Broadway" with a highly competent professional residential theater group performing before a house that can seat up to four hundred. In addition to the theater, guests at Allenberry can enjoy trout fishing on the property, the several well-maintained Har-Tru tennis courts, swimming in the olympic-size pool, volleyball, badminton, and a choice of entertainment in several lounges every evening. There are outdoor barbecues and daily buffets for those who prefer more informal eating than that at the Carriage House.

Accommodations: 60 rooms with private bath. *Driving Instructions:* The resort is on Route 174 about 6 miles southeast of Carlisle, about equidistant from Routes 34 and 74.

Canadensis, Pennsylvania

THE OVERLOOK INN

Dutch Hill Road, Canadensis, PA 18325. 717-595-7519. *Innkeepers:* Robert and Laura Tupper. Open all year.

This large old inn, built in 1860, sits on 15 acres of hilly, peaceful forests, open meadows, and mountain shrubbery such as the Poconos' magnificent mountain laurel and rhododendron. Guests at the inn can hike or ski the well-marked trails through the wooded hillside. Lolly Tupper laid the trails out herself, and there is a printed guide for one's own private tour. The Overlook Inn, as a resort, provides plenty of activities for sports-minded guests. There are the olympic-size swimming pool, badminton, shuffleboard, and boccie on the property and many more formal sports just over the mountain, such as downhill skiing, tennis, and golf. The inn recently added a lodge-conference center with five guest rooms completely separate from the inn itself.

Inside the inn are many comfortable antique-filled rooms. The guest rooms are attractively homey, with beds covered by colorful hand-crocheted throws and pretty hand-covered throw pillows, along with a blend of Victorian oak typical of a hundred-year-old inn, the modern necessities, and comfy home-made accessories. The public rooms are large, bright, and airy. Guests may relax by a roaring fire in the living room where tea and cocktails are served in the late afternoons. There is a library for the guests' use as well as several dining rooms and Tupper's Tavern.

The Overlook Inn is a popular eating spot. Chef Joseph Viberick adores cooking and will be seen popping in and out to check on diners' contentment. He also does all the baking here, including little individual loaves of bread on each table and the cheesecakes and fresh fruit pies. The dining rooms are open to the public for dinner only. The chef, by the way, canes all the antique chairs and fashions the unique table lanterns in the dining rooms.

Accommodations: 21 rooms with private bath. *Pets and Children:* Not permitted. *Driving Instructions:* The inn is 15 miles north of Stroudsburg. Take Route 447 for ¼ mile past the town of Canadensis, turn right on Dutch Hill Road. The inn is 1½ miles up the hill.

Coventryville, Pennsylvania

Coventryville is a tiny village on Route 23 just west of route 100, south of Pottstown. The village is in the northern part of historic Chester County and is an easy drive from *Valley Forge National Park*. That 2,200-acre park, the site of General George Washington's winter encampment, now has restored buildings, soldiers' huts, and cannon emplacements. Also in the Coventryville area is *Yellow Springs*, near the village of Chester Springs. Yellow Springs is the site of an eighteenth-century mineral-water spa visited by many famous Americans. St. Peters Village, on St. Peters Road, is a restored Victorian village along French Creek that has scores of stores, including craft shops. South of *Valley Forge* is the *Devon Horse Show Grounds*, site of one of the country's largest horse shows, held every May. The *Pottsgrove Mansion* in Pottstown is the distinguished Georgian home of the founder of that town, a wealthy iron-master.

COVENTRY FORGE INN

Route 23, Coventryville, Pennsylvania. Mailing address: RFD–2, Pottstown, PA 19464. 215-469-6222. *Innkeeper:* Wallis Callahan. Open late January until just before Christmas.

Coventry Forge Inn is actually a pair of early American houses one of which serves as a restaurant while the other provides lodgings, with the restaurant housed in a building that dates from 1717. Originally constructed as a chestnut-log house, it was added onto in stone by the current owner in 1938. The early construction of the log home was carefully done, with precise fitting and mortaring with plaster, which may account for the building's survival into this century. The exterior is currently covered with white stucco.

As you enter the inn, the hallway is flanked by two small dining rooms that are distinguished by their fine pine paneling. The red room to the right has painted paneling and an old fireplace that has been fitted with a rare working example of an early Franklin stove probably made by an early Coventry ironmaster who acquired the manufacturing rights from Ben Franklin, a frequent visitor to his home. The dining room to the left has unpainted paneling and a pair of matching built-in corner cupboards that flank the fireplace. The inn.has a small bar in what used to be the kitchen. This room retains its original walk-in fireplace, originally used for all cooking in the house. To the rear of the building is a newer closed-in porch, which is a popular additional dining area.

Much of the fame of the Coventry Forge Inn derives from its French restaurant. The simple and elegant menu contains enough selections to please a broad audience and yet few enough items to ensure careful preparation. The eight appetizers include trout with beurre blanc, pâté, coquilles Saint-Jacques, celery rémoulade, and salmon troisgros. There are three regular soups (onion soup, vichyssoise, and cream of watercress soup). The entrées contain very few surprises but are a classic selection of the most popular French dinner dishes. One finds duck à l'orange, steak au poivre, sweetbreads in Madeira, veal scallops in cream, roast lamb, poached bass, and several others. The list of desserts is equally classic. This restaurant has appeared on several lists of the top restaurants in the country. With its attention to detail and its care in preparation, it is easy to see why.

Guest quarters are in a similarly stuccoed house dating from 1806 located 200 yards down a private driveway. The guest house has somewhat more classic lines than the inn and is on a pleasantly landscaped property adjacent to the village church. Downstairs are a reception room and a large living room that has a pretty fireplace, which cannot be used. Upstairs are large guest rooms, each of which has a huge bathroom with tub, shower, and bidet. Three of the rooms have double beds, and two have twins. The rooms have views of the surrounding gardens and rolling pastures. The price of a room includes a Continental breakfast served on the porch dining room of the inn.

Accommodations: 5 rooms with private bath. *Pets:* Not permitted. *Driving Instructions:* Drive south on Route 100 from Pottstown for 5 miles; then go 1½ miles west on Route 23 to the inn.

Ephrata, Pennsylvania

SMITHTON

900 West Main, Ephrata, PA 17522. 717-733-6094. *Innkeeper:* Dorothy Graybill. Open all year.

In 1763 Henry Miller built and began to operate his inn and tavern at this location. Miller's tavern, known today as Smithton, stands on a hill overlooking the Ephrata Cloister and the town of Ephrata. Its walls are of brown sandstone and are a full 30 inches thick.

The first floor has a center hall with a Great Room and library to the right and a dining room and kitchen to the left. The fireplace in the Great Room has a fire going every day during cool months. The library is available for the use of guests, and breakfast is served in the sunny dining room with dark brown walls and red velvet draperies.

Upstairs, the guest rooms are large, bright, and sunny with large windows and are furnished with antique beds or handmade four-posters, some with full curtaining, bed steps, and trundle beds. Each room has a comfortable sitting area with a table, chairs, and a reading lamp. Nightshirts are provided for guests, and puffy down pillows, handmade quilts, and braided rugs make the rooms particularly inviting. A nightcap of cookies, hot cider, chocolate, or herb tea is served by firelight before bedtime.

Accommodations: 4 rooms, 2 with private bath. *Driving Instructions:* The inn is 11 miles north of Lancaster on Route 222.

EVERMAY-ON-THE-DELAWARE

River Road, Erwinna, PA 18920. 215-294-9100. *Innkeepers:* Fred Cresson, Ron Strausse, and Shirley Strausse. Open all year.

Evermay is a handsome three-story Victorian mansion whose origin goes back more than a century before the Victorian era. Built in stages beginning in the early eighteenth century, Evermay was an elegant, popular country hotel from 1871 through the early 1930s. At that time it was host to many distinguished guests that included members of the Barrymore family. Evermay reopened its doors in 1982 after a painstaking renovation that included guest rooms with private baths.

The care that has gone into restoring Evermay is evident as you approach the inn on its circular driveway. Painted autumnal gold and tan, the inn is surrounded by 25 acres of maintained grounds overlooking the Delaware River and Canal. Inside, the inn's parlor reflects stately elegance with its two fireplaces, handsome grandfather clock, and brocade camelback settees. Bouquets grace the tables here, where tea is served at 4 o'clock each afternoon and sherry is served each evening. At the rear of the mansion is a glass conservatory where a Continental breakfast is served to guests. As we sat one morning enjoying a cup of coffee, a half-dozen peacocks could be seen strolling through the backyard. Occasionally one would come up to our window and peer in inquisitively.

On the floors above, the guest rooms have been restored with Oriental rugs, walnut beds, marble-topped dressers, antique pillows, and quilts the rule. Some rooms retain their original fireplaces. In addition to the rooms in the main building, the Carriage House has a two-bedroom suite with sitting room and bath on the second floor, as well as two guest rooms downstairs.

Accommodations: 14 rooms with private bath. *Pets and Children:* Not permitted. *Driving Instructions:* The inn is on River Road (Route 32) about 12 miles north of New Hope.

THE GOLDEN PHEASANT INN

River Road, Erwinna, PA 18920. 215-294-9595. *Innkeepers:*
Ralph Schneider and Reid Pery. Open mid-February through mid-
December.

The Golden Pheasant inn actually consists of two buildings in which
overnight guests are housed. It was built in 1857 to serve the barge
traffic carrying goods from Easton to Bristol, Pennsylvania. The
fieldstone inn was bought by its current owners and fully restored in
1967. It contains six guest rooms, one of which has twin beds and a
Franklin stove. The rest have double beds. All are carpeted and
furnished with Victorian antiques including large carved beds
complemented by marble-top washstands and bureaus, floral

wallpapers, and lace curtains. Rooms on the east side of the building overlook the Delaware River; those on the west, Theodore Roosevelt State Park and the historic Delaware Canal.

The Stover Mansion, a few minutes from the inn by car, better suits the "early to bed" crowd who might be irritated by the sounds of the dining room in the main inn. The mansion was built in 1810 by the owners of one of Bucks County's best grist and lumber mills, across the street. Three of Stover Mansion's eight guest rooms have fireplaces, as do the kitchen, dining room, and living room, and all are furnished with antiques and period furniture. Oriental, braided, and hooked rugs cover the highly polished, random-width pine floors. Doors and paneling throughout the house are all of cherry cut in one of the Stover mills. Remodeled about 1890, the Federal brick structure now has an intricately pedimented gingerbread front porch and a many-dormered mansard roof.

No matter which building you stay in, request a dining table in the inn's plant-filled greenhouse dining room. In fact, it is this restaurant that draws many visitors to the inn for the first time. It serves Continental food of distinction, which does not come at a low price. You will be able to choose from a menu that changes twice a year. At last examination, some starters were escargots à la Faison, Fire Island deviled clams, avocado and shrimp, and potage velouté champignons. These were followed by a choice of one of seven entrées that included tournedos with green Madagascar peppers, smoked rib eye of beef, chicken curry, pheasant (golden, we trust), and duckling à l'orange. A list of daily specials might also include charcoal-broiled venison steak, creamed sweetbreads, or sautéed sea trout. Dinner may be taken either in the Solarium or in the inside room, which has velvet love seats, Tiffany lamps, and cut flowers. Before dinner it is pleasant to sit on the veranda with its white wicker furniture and hanging plants.

Accommodations: 14 rooms with shared baths. *Pets:* Not permitted. *Driving Instructions:* The inn is 17 miles north of New Hope on Route 32 (River Road), beside the Delaware River.

Fairfield, Pennsylvania

FAIRFIELD INN AND GUEST HOUSE

Main Street, Fairfield, PA 17320. 717-642-5410. *Innkeeper:* David
W. Thomas. Open all year except February and early September.
The Fairfield Inn and its environs are steeped in American history. It
was originally the plantation home of the Millers, who built its rear
portion in 1755 and the stone front portion two years later. Patrick
Henry was a frequent guest. In 1823 the stone house began its long life
as an inn, serving the dusty stagecoach travelers riding the "Great
Road" from York, Pennsylvania, to Hagerstown, Maryland. The
more well-to-do enjoyed the luxury of the upstairs sleeping rooms,
while the drovers spent the night on the floor down in the tavern.
Today's guests are more fortunate. The tavern has been carefully and
beautifully restored, offering dining and drinking facilities and two
attractive period rooms for overnight guests. A wide range of
antiques and fine pieces throughout the building encompass the
Fairfield's life-span. One guest room features a canopied bed and

early period antiques; the other appeals to lovers of Victoriana with a carved oak bedstead along with an antique brass and iron affair in a thoroughly comfortable setting. Both share hall bathrooms. Innkeeper David Thomas has been working long and hard in restoring the guest house a few doors down from the inn. This house offers guests a chance to spend a night in a totally museum-like environment. The sitting room and four guest rooms are uniquely decorated, each re-creating the atmosphere of a period in the building's history. One room has old-fashioned oak furnishings, another has a spool-and-rope bed; a third is totally Victorian.

The Fairfield Inn, a popular eating spot, is near Gettysburg and its attendant historic areas. One inn tradition began with General Lee's retreat after the defeat at Gettysburg. The women of Fairfield made up kettles of bean soup to feed the starving troops as they trudged through town on their way south. Bean soup is still being served at the inn. All three meals daily are offered to guests and the public. The menu featurs simple fare, much of it such local Pennsylvania dishes as chicken corn soup, a salty country ham, and the hands-down favorite —chicken and biscuits with honey. Other entrées include "frizzled" city ham as well as crab imperial made from an old Miller family recipe. Desserts of cakes and pies are made with such locally grown fresh fruits as Adams County cherries on cheesecake and a deep-dish apple pie that arrives at the table with a pitcher of heavy cream and a wedge of sharp Cheddar cheese. Who could ask for more?

Accommodations: 6 guest rooms sharing hall baths. *Pets and Children:* Not permitted. *Driving Instructions:* The inn is 8 miles west of Gettysburg, on Route 116.

Holicong, Pennsylvania

BARLEY SHEAF FARM

Route 202, Holicong, Pennsylvania. Mailing address: P.O. Box 66, Holicong, PA 18928. 215-794-5104. *Innkeepers:* Don and Ann Mills. Open March 1 to December 23.

The Mills family has owned Barley Sheaf Farm for the past several years, using it as a home for themselves and their three teenage children. After a recent trip to England, where they stayed in a number of English farms and country inns, the Millses decided to convert their home into an inn.

The mansard-roofed stone farmhouse sits at the end of a long, straight, maple-shaded driveway. Sheep graze in the pastures along the way. The farmhouse, built in 1740, is ringed by tall old trees, gardens, and a sweep of lawn. Just a few steps across the courtyard outside the main entrance stands a tall, aging, but handsome barn. This 30-acre Bucks County farm just minutes away from New Hope and the Delaware River well deserves its appointment to the National Register of Historic Sites.

Guests stay in the antique-filled bedrooms of the main house or in the little cottage at the edge of the courtyard. It would be hard to pick a room at Barley Sheaf Farm. The cottage rooms all have sloping eaves, hooked rugs, antique pine furnishings, and old-fashioned, tiny-floral-print wall coverings. Of the rooms in the farmhouse, one has a brass sleigh bed. Guests are served a large farm breakfast.

Accommodations: 9 rooms, 6 with private bath. *Pets:* Not permitted; inquire. *Driving Instructions:* Holicong is a small town on Route 202 just west of Lahaska. From the west, take Route 202 through Buckingham and Holicong to the farm just to the east.

Lancaster, Pennsylvania

NISSLY'S OLDE HOME INNS

624 West Chestnut Street, Lancaster, PA 17603. 717-392-2311 or 866-4926 (Tulpehocken). *Innkeepers:* Esther Nissly and James Henry. Open all year.

The Nissly's Olde Home Inns are quite different from others in this book. Esther Nissly and James Henry, the innkeepers of the Tulpehocken Manor and Plantation in Myerstown (listed below), have restored several Victorian homes in the heart of historic Lancaster. These four homes each contain an assortment of guest room-efficiency apartment arrangements. Three of the homes are large Victorian brick townhouses. Two of them come complete with round turrets and fancy porches; the other is more austere. The fourth house, the five-room Carriage House in the rear garden of one of the Victorians, is rented as a unit (two-day minimum) with living room, kitchen, and several bedrooms accommodating up to ten people. All rooms and apartments are air-conditioned, some have kitchenettes, some private baths, and all offer a good, fun, economical way to stay and enjoy this historic area.

The shades of former glory are still visible. The main house has stained leaded-glass windows, hand-carved woodwork, Tiffany-type chandeliers, Oriental rugs, and the original carved-oak staircases. The office is in this building. The staff will arrange for guests' pickup at the train or bus station (if convenient) and will also take interested guests up to see the Tulpehocken Manor in Myerstown. Tour buses of the Hershey-Amish area will stop at the office by reservation. The guest homes are within an easy walk of the town's many tourist facilities such as stores, restaurants, farmers' markets, and historic sites.

Accommodations: A variety, from a one-room apartment to the 5-room Carriage House. *Driving Instructions:* Go first to the office at 624 West Chestnut Street, Lancaster. It is in the center of town.

WITMER'S INN

2014 Old Philadelphia Pike, Lancaster, PA 17602. 717-299-5305. *Innkeeper:* Brant E. Hartung. Open all year.

Witmer's Inn is more formally known as the "Historic 1725 Witmer's Inn" in all its designations in state, local, and national registers of historic places. The inn was built in that year by Benjamin Weitmer, an agent for the London Land Company. Somewhat fickle about the spelling of his name, he finally settled on the version used in the inn's current name. Witmer's Inn is the only pre-Revolutionary inn still accommodating travelers on the Old Philadelphia Pike, the "Gateway to the West" road. In the eighteenth century the Pike joined Lancaster — or "Hickorytown," as it was then called — with Philadelphia, and the area was the westernmost civilized outpost at that time. The inn stands today among the farms of the descendants of the region's original settlers, the Amish. Amish buggies still pass Witmer's Inn as they travel among the surrounding fields.

The inn is a three-story fieldstone structure built in the simple pioneer style of the eighteenth century. It retains its original nine-over-six windows and bubble glass, as well as much of its original flooring and built-in furniture. A surviving corner cupboard, on the first floor, is a fine example of Colonial craftsmanship. The spring under the building is still providing water for the inn today, as it did in 1725.

All of the fully restored guest rooms have working fireplaces, and firewood is provided, at a small additional charge, for use by guests. The Tavern and a number of other rooms await restoration. Each res-

toration has been painstakingly undertaken. Layer after layer of paint has been removed, and then the rooms were repainted using colors typical for the eighteenth century. Each of the rooms is furnished with antiques and is heated and air-conditioned. Baths have been added across the hall; thus they do not disturb the authentic appearance of the guest rooms.

The eastern section of the inn houses Pandora's Antiques, a shop best known for its collection of early Amish and Mennonite quilts. Within one to five miles from the inn are most of the famous Pennsylvania Dutch region's attractions, including Ephrata Cloisters, the State Railroad Museum, farm and rural-village museums, Wheatland (the home of President James Buchanan), and of course, many well-known Pennsylvania Dutch restaurants.

Accommodations: 5 rooms with shared baths. *Pets:* Not permitted. *Driving Instructions:* The inn is east of Lancaster on Route 340.

Lititz, Pennsylvania

GENERAL SUTTER INN

14 East Main Street, Lititz, PA 17543. 717-626-2115. *Innkeepers:* Joan and Richard Vetter. Open all year.

Shortly after spawning the gold rush of 1849, John Sutter fled from California, his lands having been stolen by hordes of '49ers. Suffering from arthritis, he came to Lititz seeking relief through the town's famed mineral waters. He died in 1880 and is buried not far from the inn that now bears his name. Founded in 1764 by the Moravian Church, the inn was originally known as Zum Anker (The Sign of the Anchor). Recently the building underwent a thorough renovation by innkeepers Joan and Richard Vetter and is now one of the most appealing in this Pennsylvania Dutch area of the state. A large lobby has a fireplace, medallion-backed sofas, marble-topped coffee table, and, in several corners, birds chirping in cages. Dining is available in two rooms, including the Gaslight Pub with its cranberry walls, gaslights, and antique accessories.

Upstairs, guest rooms have recently been given a new lease on life with a fine collection of antique beds and often matching chests and chairs. Air conditioning, television, and room telephones are concessions to the present. Many rooms have views of the town square. Lititz is a pretty town pleasantly removed from the commercialization of the Lancaster area.

Accommodations: 12 rooms, most with private bath. *Driving Instructions:* Lititz is at the intersection of Routes 772 and 501.

BLACK BASS HOTEL

River Road (Route 32), Lumberville, PA 18933. 215-297-5770.
Innkeeper: Herbert E. Ward. Open all year except Christmas.

The Black Bass Hotel is an old tavern overlooking the Delaware River and the historic canal. Guest rooms on the river side have the luxury of fancy iron balconies, high above the river, where complimentary breakfasts are served in warm weather. To spend a night here is to be transported back to another time, perhaps a cross between a colonial tavern and a British pub. Herb Ward purchased the hotel in 1949 and filled it with collections of antique furnishings and decorations. There is a huge collection of memorabilia of English royalty, including life-size portraits of George II, William III, and Queen Victoria in the public rooms. The dining-room tables are highly polished old slaughtering tables surrounded by a collection of chairs of all descriptions. Large exposed beams and uprights, old lantern collections including pierced tin; and small, many-paned, wavy windows half hidden by viny plants contribute to the mellow atmosphere of ages spent caring for weary travelers. The main tavern has one of the best bars anywhere — originally from Paris's fabulous Maxim's, the bar top is solid pewter. An extensive and varied menu leans toward English and traditional American dishes, and lunches and dinners are available to both lodgers and the public. The bar is very popular on weekends, when an old-time piano player comes in and everyone is encouraged to join in the singing.

The best of the very attractive guest rooms is a two-bedroom suite with living room and private bath. The furnishings of all the rooms are very comfortable with beds ranging from a four-poster, to an enormous, intricately carved bed with floor-to-ceiling headboard, to an austere maple canopy. All are covered with either antique quilts or hand-crocheted spreads. With the exception of the suite, the rooms share two hall bathrooms.

The Black Bass Hotel has a rich history starting with its beginning as a safe refuge for trappers and other hardy frontier river travelers back in the wild and woolly days of the early eighteenth century. Built in 1745, the hotel was fortified against attacks by hostile Indians. Throughout the Revolution it remained loyal to the Crown — as it

does today! Innkeeper Ward loves to point out that George Washington definitely never slept here. In 1820 the hotel was expanded to include the main tavern section. In the mid-nineteenth century the canal builders sought rest and rather rowdy relaxation here. So rowdy were the work gangs, indeed, that they set fire to the place. A quick-witted Major Fry risked life and limb and removed a large quantity of blasting powder from the basement, where it had been stored during the making of the canal. These and other stories combine with the views of the river, canal, and its bridges, and such touches as a tiny graveyard for the inn's pets — Rabbit and Puss — and blend together into an altogether pleasing atmosphere. The Black Bass Hotel is so popular that interested visitors are advised to make their reservations well in advance.

Accommodations: 7 rooms sharing 2 hall baths; one 2-bedroom suite with private bath. *Driving Instructions:* Go 7 miles north on River Road (Route 32) from New Hope.

CLIFF PARK INN

Milford, PA 18337. 717-296-6491. *Innkeepers:* The Buchanan family. Open Memorial Day through October.

You don't have to be a golfer to enjoy the Cliff Park Inn, but we suspect it helps. Nonetheless, the inn has a history dating back more than 150 years. It has been in the Buchanan family for the entire time, first a farm with a tannery where the barn is now standing. The property had a busy logging operation that supplied railroad ties for the Erie Railroad until 1910. Around the turn of the century, the old farmhouse was turned into an inn by Annie Buchanan, and it was later enlarged to its present size. The original golf course was installed in 1913; some of the original greens are still in use today. There is also a cottage on the property that sleeps eight.

The main building has been modernized over the years and currently has a variety of styles that range from old-fashioned (natural wood floors, lace tablecloths), to rustic (pine paneling), to the modern "colonial" look with scalloped edges on beds, dressers, and valences. To their credit, the innkeepers have not felt pressured to install television or telephones in the guest rooms.

Two living rooms are furnished with antiques and newer accessories. Both have fireplaces, and there are game tables for evening and bad-weather use. In the lower level is the Sand Trap Lounge, which has a bar and features live entertainment. The inn has a large wraparound porch, and one bedroom has its own sunporch attached.

The dining room has a large menu served by waitresses clad in the Buchanan family plaid. Appetizers are plentiful with selections including asparagus spears and mushrooms à la Grèque, escargots epicurean en champignons, coquilles Saint-Jacques, and a choice of four soups. Salad choices include salad continental (mixed vegetables, shrimp, swiss cheese, olives, mushrooms, and cucumbers) and tossed green salad. The menu's twenty-eight entrées include seven varieties of veal scallopine, several steaks including tournedos of beef Rossini, and numerous other chops, chicken, and seafood preparations.

Accommodations: 18 rooms with private bath. *Driving Instructions:* Take Route 206 to Milford, near exit 10 on I-84, just across the New York–New Jersey border.

Mount Joy, Pennsylvania

CAMERON ESTATE INN

Donegal Springs Road, Mount Joy, Pennsylvania. Mailing Address: R.D. #1, Box 305, Mount Joy, PA 17552. 717-653-1773. *Innkeeper:* Kelly A. Coleman. Open all year.

On a country road off the tourist-beaten track in the center of Pennsylvania Dutch country is the historic Cameron Estate Inn, once the country home of Simon Cameron, Lincoln's outspoken Secretary of War. In a moment of candor, Cameron once defined an honest politician as "one who, when bought, stays bought." Today the estate comprises 15 acres of lawns, gardens, and woods, with its own stocked trout pond. The original four-room cottage that forms the heart of the sprawling mansion was built in 1805; the remainder was added some eighty years later. Cameron Estate, one of the largest homes in wealthy Lancaster County, is listed on the National Register of Historic Places.

Cameron Estate Inn has recently been extensively renovated. The Federal-style home reflects the grandeur typical of the Victorian period. Wide halls, huge bedrooms, tall ceilings, and wide stairs are the rule. Furnishings are mainly reproductions of the Victorian era of American furniture-building, but there are some period pieces in the public rooms. Several of the baronial guest rooms have king-sized or queen-sized beds, some canopied, and a number have working paneled and marble fireplaces. A charge is made for firewood.

Meals are served to guests and the public in the inn's dining room with its candlelight service and cabbage-rose wallpapers. The menu offers Continental and American specialties, with typical entrées including medallions of beef and veal steak sauté au paprika.

Among the nearby Pennsylvania Dutch and Amish attractions is the Donegal Church, founded in 1721. Lancaster, with its many tourist attractions, is half an hour's drive away. Mount Joy, unlike some of the surrounding tourist region, retains most of its original pastoral quality.

Accommodations: 14 rooms, 8 with private bath. *Pets and children:* Not permitted. *Driving Instructions:* The inn is on Donegal Springs Road, about 3 miles west of Route 230.

Myerstown, Pennsylvania

TULPEHOCKEN MANOR INN AND PLANTATION

650 West Lincoln Avenue, Myerstown, PA 17067. 717-866-4926.
Innkeepers: Esther Nissly and James Henry. Open all year.

As you enter the plantation grounds of Tulpehocken Manor Plantation you are carried back in history more than two hundred years. The plantation is currently a 165-acre working farm that raises grain and black Angus cattle. However, the focus of a visit here is not on the surrounding farmland but on the historic buildings that are now open as guest quarters on the property. Now a National Historic Site, the manor comprises the Christopher Ley Spring House (mid-eighteenth century), the Michael Ley Mansion (1769 and 1883), and the Cyrus Sherk Pipe Smoking House (1886), all of which have overnight accommodations. Two additional historic houses on the property accept guests on a long-term basis only.

The history of the plantation dates back to 1732, when Christopher Ley came to Philadelphia from England. He soon settled in this fertile valley region known to the local Indians as Tulpehocken. The first house he constructed was a stone spring house with a vaulted arch over the spring. In time this was expanded to two floors and is now the Christopher Ley house. In a similar way his son Michael's house, originally built in 1769, was expanded in 1883–85. Here the word "expanded" does not do this home justice. Expansion in the height of the Victorian era involved taking an eight-room stone farmhouse and converting it to a twenty-seven–room manor house. Today, the house has been fully restored to its Victorian splendor, with a large collection of Victorian furniture and accessories. Most

museum collections do not have a fraction of the artifacts that adorn every wall, shelf, ceiling, and nook and cranny of this very special place. The chairs alone number in the hundreds. One count of mirrors numbered them at 164. Beds are a testimony to the craftsmen of the period. Arched doors and chandeliers abound. To explore the twenty-seven rooms is to have a lesson in living history.

On the plantation grounds you can stroll among the historic buildings. Most buildings survive from the original owner's day, the newer ones are more than a hundred years old. The early barns and more ornate Victorian additions blend into a miniature community that has somehow captured a hundred-year-old slice of history. Meals are not available at the Plantation—a pity, because it's hard to leave even for a minute. There are, however, excellent restaurants a short drive away. If there is a disadvantage to a stay here it is, oddly enough, the great historic interest and remarkable collection of antiques. It is literally a museum, and tours are held during the daylight hours. Nonetheless, these are easily evaded if the daylight hours are used for local exploration.

Accommodations: 14 rooms sharing hall bath. Several other various lodgings on the property. *Pets:* Not permitted. *Children:* Families with children usually stay in one of the houses other than the manor house. *Driving Instructions:* The inn is on Route 422, 5 miles east of Lebanon and 23 miles west of Reading.

New Hope, Pennsylvania

CENTRE BRIDGE INN

River Road, New Hope, Pennsylvania. Mailing address: P.O. Box 74, Star Route, New Hope, PA 18938. 215-862-2048. *Innkeeper:* Stephen Dugan. Open all year.

The Centre Bridge Inn, a Williamsburg Colonial structure, was built as a private estate in 1705 on the bank of the historic Delaware River. About 120 years later, the scenic Delaware Canal was put in alongside the river. Guests today can stroll the grassy canal towpath behind the inn and watch the ducks or greet the mule-drawn tour barge as it docks at the inn so its passengers can dine at the Centre Bridge Inn restaurant. The old Colonial house was badly damaged in a fire about 20 years ago. It was later painstakingly restored and transformed into an inn. The setting is peaceful and quiet.

On the main floor the atmosphere is formal with period furnishings, wallpapers, and ten-foot-high ceilings. Below this floor is the formal, tavern-like dining room with old exposed beams, low ceilings, and walk-in fireplaces where fires are kept going. In warm weather, meals are also served on the outdoor Riverside Terrace, with flowers, trees, a fountain, and river views.

Upstairs in the inn are the guest rooms, each individually decorated. One might stay in an old-fashioned wallpapered room with a comfortable quilt-covered antique brass bed and white curtains on little dormer windows or curl up in a four-poster with a crocheted canopy surrounded by period antiques and sloping dormer window walls. The rooms share the peaceful sounds of the river.

Accommodations: 9 rooms with private bath. *Children and Pets:* Not permitted. *Driving Instructions:* The inn is north of New Hope on Route 32 (River Road) at the junction with Route 263.

HOTEL DU VILLAGE

River Road, New Hope, PA 18938. 215-862-9911 or 5164. *Innkeepers:* Omar and Barbara Arbani. Open all year; restaurant closed Mondays and Tuesdays and parts of January and February. Hotel du Village sits on what was once part of a land grant from William Penn. In the late nineteenth century an elegant country estate was established on the property. Built by Caroline Wood, the manor house was surrounded by manicured grounds, high stone walls, and stables. From 1917 to 1976 the estate was the site of several preparatory schools, most notably the Solebury School's Lower Campus. The Lower Campus property was purchased from Solebury in 1976 by Omar and Barbara Arbani, who converted the buildings to their present use two years later. Set on grounds with flower-bedecked terraces and walks shaded by oak trees, the hotel occupies several of the buildings of the former estate. White Oaks, as one of the estate houses was called, is now the home of the hotel's restaurant; Appledore offers single and double rooms as well as family suites.

The main dining room at the Hotel du Village has two large fireplaces at either end of the room, one with an interesting oak-leaf motif around the hearth. Heavy, dark wood trim, beamed ceilings, and old-fashioned Royal Staffordshire china settings create an inviting mood. The Continental menu includes such specialties as sweetbreads Financière, duckling with cherries, civet villageois (crust-covered rabbit), and entrecôte au poivre.

Guest rooms are across the yard in Appledore, a converted stable. The rooms are attractively furnished with quilts and old-fashioned beds, and are decorated with small-print wallpapers. The hotel's setting also includes a swimming pool and tennis courts.

Accommodations: 20 rooms, 18 with private bath. *Pets:* Not permitted. *Driving Instructions:* The hotel is on River Road (Route 32), north of the village.

THE INN AT PHILLIPS MILL

North River Road, New Hope, PA 18938. 215-862-2984. *Innkeepers:* Joyce and Brooks Kaufman. Open all year except January to mid-February.

As you enter the Inn at Phillips Mill, you are greeted by a copper pig hanging just above the door. Although we have always suspected that it was placed there to symbolize the abandon with which we approach dining at the Mill, in truth it harks back to the inn's origins in the eighteenth century. In its youth the stone barn stood next to the village piggery and was also once a gristmill. When Joyce and Brooks Kaufman bought the property they set out to create formal yet relaxed dining areas and five intimate guest rooms. Each of these now has four-poster or brass beds with quilts, attractive wallpapers, and full bathrooms. One room is part of a suite that has its own sitting room and is available at a modest surcharge above the usual room rate. Under the eaves is our own favorite, its sloping ceiling papered in a tiny print. Foil-wrapped chocolates by Godiva were waiting on the night table.

Meanwhile, French dining awaits. The several choices here include small formal dining rooms upstairs, and downstairs a lounge with a large stone fireplace and comfortable leather lounging furniture or the glassed-in terrace with its copper roof.

Among the offerings on the evening menu might be duck à l'orange, lamb chops forestière, and a "spring garden dish for vegetarians," a thoughtful addition to the menu for the growing number of travelers who prefer not to eat meat. Starters include a pâté du chef, escargots, and seafood crepes. Guests can choose to be pampered by rising from their night's sleep to find waiting outside their door a breakfast of croissants, coffee cake, jam, and coffee.

Accommodations: 4 rooms and 1 suite, all with private bath. *Pets:* Not permitted. *Driving Instructions:* The inn is 1½ miles north of New Hope on Route 32 (River Road).

LOGAN INN

Main Street, New Hope, PA 18938. 215-862-5134. *Innkeepers:* Carl Lutz and Arthur Sanders. Open mid-February through December 31.

The Logan Inn, established in 1727, is the oldest building in New Hope. It has been host to travelers along the "Old York Road" for more than 250 years. In the early days of New Hope, the village was largely owned by John Wells, a carpenter from Philadelphia. Wells operated the local ferry across the Delaware River and started his Ferry Tavern (later the Logan Inn) a few years later. For several years the town was called Wells' Ferry. Subsequently, the village was renamed each time the ferrymaster changed. When Washington and his high-ranking officers bivouacked there in 1776, the tavern was the scene of the final planning of the Americans' attack on Trenton,

which originated with the famed crossing of the Delaware on Christmas Day. The name "New Hope" was given the village by Benjamin Parry after a fire had destroyed his gristmills. When he rebuilt the mills, he named them New Hope Mills, giving rise at once to the new name for the village. The Logan Inn received its current name in the 1820s, when the town erected on the inn's lawn a metal statue of the Delaware Indian chief Wingohoking, who was also called Chief Logan, a name he had chosen for himself out of admiration for William Penn's secretary, James Logan. In more recent times the inn served as off-Broadway headquarters for the old Algonquin Round Table crowd; it has played host to Moss Hart, Richard Rodgers and Lorenz Hart, Dorothy Parker, Marc Connelly, Helen Hayes, Tallulah Bankhead, Celeste Holm, and Liza Minnelli.

The Logan Inn is filled with antiques and fine paintings. Its taproom has a collection of antique steins. An 1839 portrait of the young Prince Albert, painted the year before he married Queen Victoria, gazes down from one wall. There is a sizable collection of old clocks and many other pieces throughout the public and guest rooms. The bedrooms are also furnished with antiques, such as brass beds, carved Lincoln-type high wooden bedsteads, marble-topped dressers, and armoires. Many lamps in the guest rooms have been adapted from antique vases or figurines.

The main dining room is the attractive glass-roofed conservatory, where one dines under the stars and amid orchids, ferns, and bromeliads in all four seasons. The menu offers a selection of dishes varying from restaurant standards to specialties rarely seen on the menus of other inns. Appetizers range from tomato juice to salmon mousse or caviar crepe à la Russe. There are three daily soups, followed by a choice of fourteen entrées: The old standards are represented by chopped sirloin, lamb chops, filet mignon, sweetbreads, sauerbraten, broiled chicken, and chicken Kiev, among others. The shrimp Logan (with dill, butter, and wine), Swedish lamb Bernadotte, and veal piquante are among the more adventurous dishes offered. Desserts include the inn's famous chocolate rum pie, Swedish apple pie, and a hot apple-nut cake with hot-buttered-rum sauce.

Accommodations: 10 rooms, 8 with private bath. *Pets:* Not permitted. *Driving Instructions:* The inn is in the center of town near the village square (where the cannon is).

PINEAPPLE HILL

River Road, Box 34C R.D. 2, New Hope, PA 18938. 215-862-9608.
Innkeepers: Mary and Stephen Darlington. Open all year.
This old-farmhouse-turned-bed-and-breakfast-inn stands on a knoll overlooking a bend in a country road near New Hope in Pennsylvania's Bucks County. The pineapple on the inn's sign as well as its bright-red paneled front door beckon invitingly to travelers. The hall just inside leads to an appealing farmhouse parlor displaying antique country pine furniture, old quilts, and braided rugs. On the other side of the hall is a second sitting room, with a big bay window where antique green bottles glow in the sunlight. Pewter is displayed in an old cupboard, and the brick hearth is flanked by wing chairs. Another old quilt is draped over a carriage bench in the nook by the window, and a harvest table stands under a tin candle chandelier.

An old staircase leads to the guest rooms, with their hand-stenciled curtains and antique quilts and linens. One room has pineapple wallpaper, a carriage bench, and a spindle bed; another boasts a Victorian oaken bedstead tucked under sloping eaves. On the lawn out back is a swimming pool set inside the ruins of a stone barn.

Breakfast at Pineapple Hill includes home-baked breads, croissants, cookies, pies, and cakes accompanied by your choice of assorted teas or coffee. Sherry is served in the evening, before bedtime.

Accommodations: 4 rooms with shared baths. *Pets:* Not permitted. *Driving Instructions:* 4 miles south of New Hope on Route 32.

THE WEDGWOOD INN

111 West Bridge Street, New Hope, PA 18938. 215-862-2570. *Innkeepers:* Nadine Silnutzer and Carl Glassman. Open all year.
Just two blocks up the hill from town, along a shaded winding road lined with antique shops and inviting little boutiques, stands the Wedgwood Inn. This hip-gabled Victorian, built in 1870, has a wraparound porch with turned posts and scrolled brackets. Hanging ferns, pots of flowers, and garden-lined walks attest to the innkeepers' horticultural talents.

The Wedgwood Inn, a guesthouse for more than thirty years, was given a new lease on life recently when the Glassmans purchased the building and renovated it from stem to stern, filling their new inn with family antiques and an ever growing collection of Wedgwood pottery. The sitting room just off the porch is a pleasant spot to relax by the tall bay windows and enjoy light classical music. Crisp organdy curtains and cream-colored walls are set off by pots of ferns and the woodwork's Wedgwood-blue trim. All the rooms are cooled by old-fashioned paddle fans on the high ceilings. One of the guest rooms has a graceful four-poster bed complete with a lace canopy. A spray of fresh flowers on the night table and a quilt draped over the foot of the bed add appeal. Another room has a spool bed and lots of ruffles, and

yet another has an iron bedstead covered with a patchwork quilt. Fresh flowers and Victorian antiques are the rule at the Wedgwood, and complimentary carafes of Amaretto are provided for guests' enjoyment. Breakfasts of freshly squeezed orange juice, home-baked breads and muffins, and, occasionally, fresh fruit salad are served on the sun porch or in bed, if guests so desire.

The innkeepers, Carl and Dee, are experts on the New Hope area, and the sitting room is filled with books and pamphlets on local sights and activities. New Hope is well known for its warm-weather attractions, but a not very well kept secret here is the romance of wintertime with its cross-country skiing, sledding, Christmas festivals, and ice-skating on the canal.

Accommodations: 8 rooms, 2 with private bath. *Driving Instructions:* Take Route 179 two blocks south of the Lambertville bridge. The Wedgwood Inn is at the top of the hill, on the left.

Newfoundland, Pennsylvania

BUENA VISTA FAMILY RESORT

Route 447, Newfoundland, PA 18445. 717-676-3800. *Innkeepers:* Al and Ruth Seifert. Open all year.

Buena Vista is a small family resort on 75 acres of Pocono hillside. The century-old barn on the property (now outfitted with a wood-burning stove and used for indoor games) is all that remains of the original Moravian settlement there. The remaining buildings date from just after the turn of the century and have been operated as a resort since World War II. Elevations at Buena Vista range from 1,700 to 1,800 feet, providing cool summer evenings, invigorating fall days, and abundant snowfall for winter sports.

The resort's main lodge is a clapboard building set on a typical Pennsylvania stone foundation. Its dining room and several guest rooms on the second floor overlook the resort's small farm pond. Also in this building are the gift shop and lounge areas. Furnishings throughout the lodge, as well as in the two other similar buildings that have the remaining twenty guest rooms, are simple and have a "fortyish" look—not period antiques, but not overwhelmingly modern either.

Dining at the resort is on the American Plan. A typical dinner might offer baked ham with raisin sauce, breast of turkey with gravy, roast top round of beef, or stuffed breast of chicken. Dinner selections include hot rolls, relish tray, juice or other appetizer, vegetables, dessert, and beverage. In summer, the meal also includes a trip to the salad bar. Guests frequently may choose a predinner option of hot hors d'oeuvres and fruit punch served in the lounge.

In true resort fashion, there are many fair-weather activities on the premises including craft-making, fishing, hiking, nature study, archery, badminton, baseball, basketball, croquet, football, horseshoes, table tennis, and volleyball. Most other individual sports, including golf, tennis, riding, and indoor ice skating, are available nearby.

Accommodations: 26 rooms, 23 with private bath. *Pets:* Not permitted. *Driving Instructions:* Take I-84 to exit 6 and go south on Route 507 to Route 447. The inn is one block south of the village of Newfoundland, on Route 447.

WHITE CLOUD

Route 447, Newfoundland, Pennsylvania. Mailing address: R.D. 1, Box 215, Newfoundland, PA 18445. 717-676-3162. *Innkeeper:* George Wilkinson. Open all year, but call first, especially in winter.

In 1970, George Wilkinson purchased White Cloud from previous owners who had run it as a small Poconos resort with the accent on its restaurant. His original purpose was to provide a retreat house for members of the Self-Realization Fellowship, a group that practices yoga meditation. The group used only a fraction of the space and soon realized that the remaining rooms would make an excellent inn. George decided then to open it to anyone who would appreciate a place to escape for a time from the noise and cares of the world and unwind. He opened his dining room to the public in 1975 and, since then, has had an increasing clientele of travelers and local people who enjoy eating in a unique restaurant. No meat or alcoholic beverages are served, and the emphasis here is on healthful living through healthful eating. The dining room is open to the public from May through October and to inn guests at all times.

While there is a chapel and regular meditation services, guests are welcome but in no way urged to participate. Beyond this, the inn is simply a peaceful, relaxing place. The amenities of a Poconos inn are here, including a swimming pool, tennis court, shuffleboard, and an abundance of hiking trails that start at the inn's doors. The inn owns the surrounding 50 acres.

George is particularly proud of the dining room. It serves no meat or fish and uses whole-grain flour in its baking. No artificial preservatives or additives are used, and most desserts contain no added sugar. In season the vegetables are from the inn's own organic garden. Three house specialties include cheese-nut balls in Mexican sauce, cheese bake (spinach, cottage, and cheddar cheeses baked in a casserole), baked nut loaf with mushroom sauce, and cashew soup. Various macrobiotic dishes are offered as well.

Accommodations: 20 rooms, 7 with private bath. *Driving Instructions:* The inn is on Route 447, 3 miles south of Newfoundland.

Philadelphia, Pennsylvania

SOCIETY HILL HOTEL

301 Chestnut Street, Philadelphia, PA 19106. 215-925-1394. *Innkeepers:* Judith Campbell and David DeGraff. Open all year.
Society Hill was, and remains today, a fashionable district within

Philadelphia's Old City. Over the past thirty years the area has undergone a revitalization thanks to the federal government's parks program. The Old City is steeped in America's history, and the Society Hill Hotel, built in 1832, will put visitors in the right frame of mind for forays into our nation's beginnings. This "urban inn" sits in the midst of Independence National Historical Park. The Federal Visitors Center is diagonally across the street from the hotel; Independence Hall, the city's most popular attraction, is just two blocks away.

Society Hill Hotel was totally renovated in 1980. Its historic beginnings are remembered in the fine crown moldings, hand stenciling, brass beds, and historic prints. The guest rooms have soft gray wall-to-wall carpeting and are furnished with a blend of antiques and traditional-style modern pieces. Some of the private bathrooms retain their original period brass fixtures.

A breakfast tray with freshly squeezed orange juice and warm rolls and jam is brought to each guest's room in the morning. Downstairs, the Society Hill Bar and Restaurant overlooks the Historical Park. A blackboard menu offers light lunch and dinner in a setting of light woods, stained glass, and greenery. Philadelphia cheesesteak, Roman artichoke hearts, and apple-walnut pie are house specialties.

Accommodations: 12 rooms with private bath. *Pets:* Not permitted. *Driving Instructions:* The hotel is on Chestnut Street between Third and Fourth streets.

Point Pleasant, Pennsylvania

INNISFREE

Cafferty Road, Point Pleasant, Pennsylvania. Mailing address: P.O. Box 108, Point Pleasant, PA 18950. 215-297-8329. *Innkeeper:* John R. Huestis. Open all year.

We first heard of Innisfree from our friends Tom and Sue Carroll of the Mainstay Inn in Cape May, New Jersey. Tom and Sue's taste in furnishing their own inn (which see) obviously extends to their evaluation of other inns. Innisfree is a streamside stone building built in 1748 as a gristmill for making flour and grinding cattle feed. The business was expanded by the addition of a separate saw mill (still on the property) in 1853. Powder was ground for the colonial troops at the gristmill, which continued to operate until about 1913. After a number of years of abandonment, the mill was bought and restoration began in 1959, a process that continues even today.

Accommodations are in antique-filled rooms with open-beam ceilings. All but one of these rooms face a stream whose sounds lull one to sleep. The loft room has a stone fireplace, sleep loft, library, and kitchen. The Master Bedroom, with partial paneling from an old Wall Street bank, has a marble-floored private bathroom. The Mill Room has a large fireplace, old gear wheels, and a stone "grotto" bathroom. The Studio has a tub for soaking and a view of the stream.

To step into this mill is to venture back in time. The combination of beamed ceilings, the fire in the fireplaces, and the smell of good food cooking combine to produce an atmosphere of welcome. The living room is filled with books and comfortable furniture in which to curl up before the fire or by one of the three tall windows overlooking the mill stream. In the morning, guests gather at the long antique-oak table to enjoy crepes, waffles, or breakfast soufflés prepared by innkeeper John Huestis. In the background the sound of classical music competes with the stream's own music as guests enjoy both the food and breakfast conversations.

John recently bought and renovated an old barn on the hillside above Innisfree. Three of the six guest rooms inside it have fireplaces.

John prides himself on being an American version of the most appreciated European concierge. He is always happy to spend extra time guiding guests to the most interesting local sights or recreational opportunities or to the best local antique shops or boutiques. He will also be glad to make dinner reservations at any of the area's fine inns and restaurants. Groups of eight or more should inquire about John's specially prepared dinners available with sufficient advance notice. Innisfree is a small, mellow place where guests receive the personal attention never possible in larger inns.

Accommodations: 16 rooms, 3 with private bath. *Pets:* Not permitted. *Children:* Under twelve not permitted. *Driving Instructions:* From the intersection of Routes 202 and 32 in New Hope, take River Road (Route 32) north 8 miles to Point Pleasant. Immediately after crossing the bridge, look for the left turn into Cafferty Road. Proceed 100 feet to the gravel drive on the left (a church is on the right).

SIGN OF THE SORREL HORSE

Old Bethlehem Road, Quakertown, PA 18951. 215-536-4651. *Innkeepers:* Ronald Strouse and Fred Cresson. Open all year.

This old tavern has been host to weary travelers since stagecoaches first began rolling up in the late eighteenth century. A Revolutionary War veteran was one of the first innkeepers at the Sign of the Sorrel Horse. The walls inside expose the native fieldstone from which the tavern was built. Windows with tiny wavy panes have been set into thick limestone walls. Ground floor rooms include an intimate stone-walled pub and dining rooms softly lit by candles. The heavy beams of the ceilings are exposed, and cubbyhole cutouts in the stone walls display pieces of antique china. Amid the rustic charm, a fine little French restaurant with a changing menu might offer an appetizer of snapper quennelles with shrimp sauce, or a bouchée with sweet-breads, or veal pâté followed by, perhaps, pork tapenade, lamb noisettes with green peppercorn butter, or salmon with leeks, crème fraiche, and lobster. Breakfast is served on a trellised terrace.

Up a narrow staircase is a most inviting common room where a decanter of sherry waits on an antique cupboard, and an old tapestry decorates the wall. Just off this room are the guest rooms, with their richly colored Oriental rugs scattered on wideboard pine floors. The heavy antique bedsteads and bureaus are set off nicely against the exposed stone walls; fresh fruit and flowers are set out for guests' enjoyment; and low windows offer glimpses of the shaded lawns, swimming pool, and woods beyond.

Lake Nockamixon, a state park, is just down the road from the inn. Here, guests find canoeing, sailing, swimming, and horseback riding. The innkeepers at the Sign of the Sorrel Horse provide picnic lunches for excursions into the park and surrounding Bucks County countryside. Just a few minutes from the inn are more than one hundred antique shops, the Delaware River and Canal, and the historic artists' colony of New Hope.

Accommodations: 6 guest rooms, 4 with private bath. *Pets and Children:* Not permitted. *Driving Instructions:* Take Route 563 to Old Bethlehem Road. The inn is north of 563, on the west side of the road.

THE RIEGELSVILLE HOTEL

10–12 Delaware Road, Riegelsville, PA 18077. 215-749-2469. *Innkeepers:* Fran and Harry Cregar. Open all year.

The Riegelsville Hotel, dating from 1838, stands at a curve of the road with the river in front and the canal behind it. The Riegelsville is a friendly hotel, the most rustic of the inns in the New Hope area. Exposed rough-sawn original siding and stone walls are liberally used within the hotel's public rooms.

In contrast to the rustic aspects is the superb stained-glass work displayed in both dining rooms and the pub. Derivative of the Art Nouveau movement, the panels were executed by the Cregars' son Harry, who works at the hotel as the head chef. Among his appetizers, his oyster and spinach parmesan has won praise from local critics. Among the dinner entrées are shrimps with mushrooms, flounder Roumania, New York strip steak, roast Long Island duckling, and chicken hunters-style. During the winter months a fire is kept going in both dining room fireplaces. One, an enormous cooking fireplace, still has the original bake oven used more than a century ago.

Upstairs, the rooms have an appealing informality combined with more formal touches such as four-poster or walnut high-backed beds. Several have floral-print papers and water views. Baths or half baths are right in some of the rooms, hidden by a folding screen or not at all. Other rooms are a short walk from hall baths.

Accommodations: 12 rooms, 7 with full or half baths. *Driving Instructions:* Take Route 32 to Riegelsville and turn onto River Road. The inn is next to one of the oldest Delaware River bridges.

Scenery Hill, Pennsylvania

CENTURY INN

Scenery Hill, PA 15360. 412-945-6600. *Innkeepers:* Megin and
Gordon Harrington. Open mid-March to mid-December.

Century Inn was built as a stagecoach stop in 1794 by the Hill family,
who founded the village of Scenery Hill. The inn first served travelers
on the famed Nemacolin Indian trail used by George Washington and
his troops during the French and Indian Wars. The trail later became
the historic National Road connecting the East Coast with the
Western frontier. Century Inn is one of the stone buildings that dot
the farmlands of Pennsylvania. The tans of the cut stones are highlighted by the white posts of the long porch and the trim on the high,
narrow windows with their many small, wavy panes of glass. Two
large chimneys are continuations of the stone side walls. A garden

path leads across the lawn and up to the porch, which is framed by an old-fashioned flower garden, one of many on the inn's grounds. Antique rocking chairs, potted flowers on a bench, and an old spinning wheel combine to make this an inviting place to sit and relax in the afternoon sun. Two illustrious travelers who have partaken of the hospitality here in the past were Andrew Jackson and General Lafayette. Jackson returned in 1825 on the way to his presidential inauguration. It is no surprise that the Century Inn is in the National Register of Historic Places.

In 1945, Mary and Gordon Harrington bought the inn and began their careful restoration. They are now deceased, and the inn has since been cared for by several members of the Harrington family and remains in the family to this day. A large array of rare heirloom antiques is found throughout the inn. The furnishings and decorations span decades of collecting, and the antiques themselves span centuries, some predating the eighteenth-century inn. One room relatively untouched by the march of time and guests' footsteps is a first-floor room that in earlier days was the innkeeper's own. The hand-plastered walls and woodwork are original to the builders' time. The stencils are traced from designs by Moses Eaton, one of the nation's few recognized stencilers from the early nineteenth century.

The old keeping room's large fireplace is hung with unusual kitchen articles from the eighteenth and nineteenth-centuries. It is one of five very popular dining rooms at Century Inn, famed nationwide for its cuisine and décor. The innkeepers receive many requests to view the historic rooms and it is often possible now to tour the second-floor rooms with the Harringtons' permission. One room upstairs contains a collection of antique dolls displayed in a period bedroom with old quilts, rug, and four-poster bedstead. Comfortable rooms available to overnight guests carry out the inn's theme and the atmosphere of colonial times. Because of the inn's popularity, reservations must be made well in advance to avoid disappointment for both lodgings and dinners.

Accommodations: 6 rooms, 5 with private bath. *Pets:* Not permitted. *Driving Instructions:* The inn is 12 miles east of Washington, Pennsylvania, on Route 40 (the old National Road).

THE INN AT STARLIGHT LAKE

Starlight, PA 18461. 717-798-2519. *Innkeepers:* Jack and Judy McMahon. Open all year except April 1–15.

The Inn at Starlight Lake dates from the turn of the century, an era when tourists from Pennsylvania, New York, and New Jersey would take the old Ontario and Western Railway directly to the town and the inn. The depot is still standing, and Starlight Falls, over which the track ran, is still enjoyed by guests at the inn. At the edge of the lake is the sprawling, rustic, Adirondack-style lodge. There is also the Family House (1956) and three cottage-like structures. Attention focuses on Starlight Lake itself and its waterfront recreation. The surrounding countryside is largely unspoiled, with hiking most of the year and cross-country skiing in winter.

Public rooms at the inn are large, with comfortable chairs and a smattering of antiques, including chairs, sideboards, mirrors, prints, and tables. The dining room overlooks the lake, and both the lobby and the Stovepipe Bar have fireplaces. Guest rooms are all different, some with twin beds, some with doubles, some connecting rooms with bath between, forming suites. One of the cottage-like houses has a fireplace.

A short road separates the inn from the lake, where there are a dock and a long pier where boats are moored. There are a swimming raft, sitting area, croquet court, basketball area, shuffleboard court, horseshoe area, and small children's playground area, plus a clay tennis court. The inn is 5 miles from the Delaware River, with its excellent fishing and canoeing. In winter there is cross-country skiing on the grounds of the inn.

The dining room is open for all three meals to the public as well as guests. The dinner menu has choices of about twelve entrées, of which Wiener schnitzel and Jäger schnitzel are house specialties, along with steaks, ham, lobster, shrimp, a daily chicken choice, plus several daily specials such as a prime rib roast or an Italian dish.

Accommodations: 30 rooms, 20 with private bath. *Pets:* Not permitted. *Driving Instructions:* From New York, take Route 17 to Hancock, then Route 191 south to Route 370. Turn right and proceed 3.5 miles. The inn's sign is on Route 370, a mile from the inn.

Upper Black Eddy, Pennsylvania

BRIDGETON HOUSE

River Road, Upper Black Eddy, PA 18972. 215-982-5856. *Innkeepers:* Beatrice and Charles Briggs. Open all year.

Bridgeton House, a riverfront country inn on the Delaware, is a restored roadside inn that re-creates the style of the early nineteenth century. Standing at the Pennsylvania end of the bridge to Milford, New Jersey, it has crisply painted white brickwork punctuated by dark red shutters.

Inside, guests may enjoy the inn's large living room, with its braided rugs and primitive furniture that includes a handsome antique tavern table and twig chairs. There is one guest room on this floor, with tall French doors that afford a view to the river and the bridge. Its canopied bed is a well-executed reproduction by a local craftsman. Upstairs, several of the six guest rooms also have river views, and most have four-poster beds, puffy quilts, painted floors, exposed beams, and antique accessory furnishings. All in all, the inn is a tribute to what can be done to create the mood of a much earlier era.

Accommodations: 7 rooms with private bath. *Smoking:* Not permitted. *Pets:* Not permitted. *Children:* Not encouraged. *Driving Instructions:* The inn is on River Road (Route 32).

West Virginia

Berkeley Springs, West Virginia

THE COUNTRY INN

207 South Washington Street, Berkeley Springs, WV 25411. 304-258-2210. *Innkeepers:* Jack and Adele Barker. Open all year.

The Country Inn adjoins the historic mineral springs and baths of Berkeley Springs, better known as Bath, West Virginia. The attractive, rather formal-looking structure was built in 1932 to house visitors to the famous health spa that adjoins the inn. The style of the inn is colonial: Six tall white columns dominate the face of the three-story brick building. On summer evenings guests can sit and relax here in the many high ladder-back rockers on the porch. The inn overlooks the town, with its springs, commons, bandstand, and brook. Visitors must cross the brook to get to the hotel.

The inn's interior is pleasant; the public rooms are bright and inviting, warmed by two wood-burning stoves on chilly evenings. The center of the inn is the living room, with its comfortable couches and chairs and such touches as fresh flowers in summer and dried-flower arrangements in winter. Just off this room is the Country Gallery, a high-ceilinged lounge with overstuffed chairs, rockers, and card tables. This room has antique throw rugs on the hardwood floors and some of the Barkers' family antiques. On the other side of the living room is the Morgan Room, a small country store for guests and visitors.

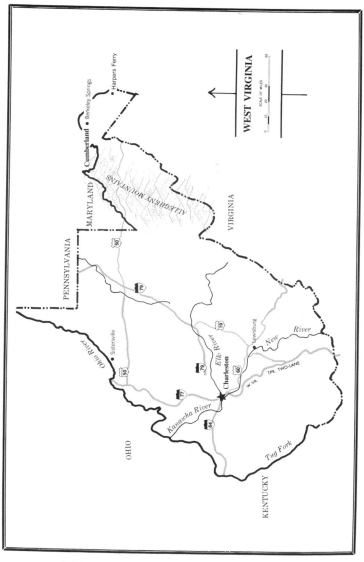

Each guest room is decorated differently, most with wooden furniture and color television. The honeymoon suite contains a large brass bed.

The West Virginia Room is the attractive main dining room. The dark wood panels, white walls, trestle tables, and reproduction Windsor chairs evoke an atmosphere of colonial times. The menu features West Virginia country cooking: ham with red-eye gravy, golden brown pan-fried trout (fillets), and hot, freshly baked pies and pastries. The breakfasts will fortify the heartiest of eaters: buttermilk pancakes with southern ham or sausage, omelets, eggs Benedict, and steaming hot coffee. There are daily cooks' specials posted for each meal. A favorite dining spot is the "country garden," where meals are served amid plants and hanging baskets of flowers. The Country Inn is the perfect place to stay while partaking of the Berkeley Springs hot mineral baths, massages, heat treatments, and saunas. The Roman Baths are the most fun; each bath is an individual tiled sunken pool with 750 gallons of regulated hot mineral water. There are fourteen of these in the park. The Berkeley Springs have been enjoyed by millions since the Indians first discovered the curative powers of the water. America's oldest health spa, this is now in the National Register of Historic Places.

Accommodations: 37 rooms, 23 with private bath. *Driving Instructions:* Go 6 miles south on Route 522 from Hancock, Maryland, at the I-70 interchange. The inn is in the center of Berkeley Springs.

THE OLD INN LODGE

Cacapon State Park, Berkeley Springs, WV 25411. 304-258-1022.
Open in spring, summer and fall only.

Cacapon State Park is part of the excellent state park system of West Virginia. Almost all parks there have excellent accommodations and restaurants run by the state. In all, there are thirteen vacation parks plus many day-use parks. Most vacation parks are actually state-owned resorts, led by the excellence of Pipestem.

Owing to their size, the other parks have not been included in this book. Cacapon is the sole exception because of its Old Inn Lodge. The Old Inn was built of rough-hewn logs, and it recaptures a colonial atmosphere with its hand-wrought hardware, stone chimneys, and veranda. The rooms, paneled in chestnut and knotty pine, are small and low-ceilinged as in pre-Revolutionary times and have old-fashioned shared or connecting baths. In addition to the eleven rustic rooms in the old lodge, there are twenty-nine cabins suitable for family vacations and fifty rooms in the modern Cacapon Lodge overlooking the golf course designed by Robert Trent Jones. The latter lodge will appeal to those who wish a state park setting with modern accommodations complete with air-conditioning, television, telephone, and bath.

Cacapon is an attractive park with a large freshwater beach offering swimming, fishing, and boating; golf, horseback riding, picnicking, tennis, croquet, volleyball, basketball, shuffleboard, badminton, and horseshoes are also available. There are a resident naturalist and several nature programs and hiking trails. Extremely popular is hiking up Cacapon Mountain in the park. In summer, all these organized activities attract large numbers of people; so those desiring a peaceful setting should come during the week to avoid weekend crowds. There is a large restaurant with banquet rooms in Cacapon Lodge. Visitors who wish to take advantage of the famous Berkeley Springs need only drive to the day-use park at the hot springs to avail themselves of the swimming, mineral baths, roman baths, and assorted treatments offered there.

Accommodations: 11 rooms in Old Inn Lodge; 29 cabins; 50 rooms in Cacapon Lodge. *Pets:* Not permitted in any state park lodges. *Driving Instructions:* Take either Route 9 or Route 522 to Berkeley Springs. The park is south of Berkeley Springs off Route 522.

Lewisburg, West Virginia

GENERAL LEWIS MOTOR INN

301 East Washington Street, Lewisburg, WV 24901. 304-645-2600.
Innkeeper: Colonel Charles May. Open all year.

At some time in its past, the General Lewis Inn began to call itself the
General Lewis Motor Inn. Such a name is more than likely to frighten
away the more loyal country-inn lover, so we hasten to assure you that

this is the genuine article. The inn's earliest section dates from 1798 and now serves as the dining room. The remainder of the inn was built in 1929 and maintains the look of the original inn rooms. Here is a country inn that can and does serve as a museum piece, with as fine an antique collection as you would see in most village historical museums. The central lobby has exposed beams and a working fireplace adorned with white mantelpiece and an old mantel clock. At the front a long, shaded veranda has heavy, tall columns supporting its roof, which offers protection to guests who wish to sit outside on the numerous old-fashioned rockers. Even here on the veranda the overnight guest is apt to find one of the owner's antiques, such as an old spinning wheel. Each of the guest rooms is decorated individually, but all retain the look of yesteryear. Some have a pair of four-poster beds, one has a canopy bed, some have fireplaces (nonfunctioning), and all have antique accessories that complete the country-inn look. Modern conveniences include telephones, air conditioning, and television in each room.

The inn's dining room is open for breakfast and dinner to guests and the public daily, as well as for the Sunday noontime meal. The accent is on plain cooking with a West Virginia touch. Diners may choose from several appetizers, including juice, fresh fruit in season, and the soup of the day. This is followed by a choice of entrée from a list of from five to seven available daily. Selections include country fried chicken, fried country ham, pork chops, filet mignon, T-bone steak, and a fish dish. The meal includes the appetizer, entrée and two vegetables, hot rolls, and coffee or tea. Dessert is extra. Prices for the complete dinner except dessert are reasonable.

Accommodations: 28 rooms with private bath. *Pets:* Permitted, with a small additional charge. *Driving Instructions:* Take the Lewisburg exit off I-64.

Lewisburg is a town of about 2,500 just off Route I-64 in the southeastern corner of the state, near the Virginia border. Lewisburg is an attractive and historic gaslighted town named for a Revolutionary War leader, General Lewis. It has a Confederate cemetery and a recently restored *Old Stone Church*, built in 1796, with white cupola and black shutters. The church is open daily except Thanksgiving and Christmas.

WELLS INN

316 Charles Street, Sistersville, WV 26175. 304-652-3111. *Innkeeper:* Martha McGinnis. Open all year.

Sistersville was a sleepy village of 300 until shortly before the turn of the century, when the "Pole Cat" oil well was drilled, tapping one of the richest fields in the country. Overnight, 2,500 oil and natural-gas wells sprang up and the town's population ballooned to 15,000. The Wells Hotel sprang up with them. It was built in 1894 by Ephraim Wells, grandson of the founder of Sistersville. The hotel was hostess in those bawdy, colorful days to visiting oil tycoons, politicians, and traveling troupes of entertainers who performed at the elaborate Sistersville Opera House. As those glamorous days faded, so did the old hotel. It had a brief flurry of remodeling in 1929, when the bathrooms were added. In 1965, John Wells Kinkaid purchased his grandfather's old hotel and restored it to its rather gaudy "boom town" splendor. Renamed the Wells Inn, it is now listed in the National Register of Historic Places.

The lobby has gold flowered wallpaper accented by the original dark mahogany woodwork and red carpeting. The center of the room has a big white fountain, and the registration desk is of dark mahogany lit by beaded and leaded glass lamps and wall sconces. A brass cuspidor, leaded-glass phone booth, and a crank phone add to the atmosphere of an era gone by. Just off the lobby is the Victorian parlor, presided over by a portrait of old Ephraim and a floor-to-ceiling grandfather clock (and these ceilings are high). This room has the same red carpeting, as well as flocked wallpapers. Victorian furnishings and lights are used throughout. Which plant would one expect to find in an ornate Victorian establishment? The hardy Boston fern, of course. And here it is. There are scrolled tables topped with marble, velvet love seats and chairs, hanging chandeliers, and ornate framed mirrors and oils.

The main dining room has old lighting fixtures, including chandeliers, from the Sistersville Opera House and the old Wells building. The tables are covered with white cloths, and the Victorian chairs are of emerald-green tufted velvet and carved wood. The dining rooms are open to the public for all meals. Downstairs is the Wooden

Derrick Club, the inn's pub. Its sandstone-block walls are painted gold, and it is decorated with advertising art, old pictures, and an ornate upright piano.

The bedrooms are furnished with new brass beds and some period pieces. During the inn's restoration, phones, television, wall-to-wall carpeting, and air conditioning were added. The Governor's Suite has a drawing room filled with gold-velvet chairs, marble-topped tables, and dried-flower arrangements. The bed is hidden behind golden drapes, which one draws back on retiring. This inn is a fine place to don your top hat or ostrich plumes and spend an evening back in great-grandmother's time.

Accommodations: 36 rooms with private bath. *Pets:* Permitted, but guests are responsible for any damage they cause. *Driving Instructions:* Sistersville is about 40 miles south of Wheeling on Route 2, which runs along the Ohio River.

Index of Inns

WITH ROOM-RATE AND CREDIT-CARD INFORMATION

Inns are listed in the chart that follows. In general, rates given are for two persons unless otherwise stated. Single travelers should inquire about special rates. The following abbreviations are used throughout the chart:

dbl. = double. These rates are for two persons in a room.

dbl. oc. = double occupancy. These rates depend on two persons being registered for the room. Rentals of the room by a single guest will usually involve a different rate basis.

EP = European Plan: no meals.

MAP = Modified American Plan: rates include dinner and breakfast. Readers should confirm if stated rates are per person or per couple.

AP = American Plan: rates include all meals. Readers should confirm if stated rates are per person or per couple.

BB = Bed and Breakfast: rates include full or Continental breakfast.

Credit-Card Abbreviations

AE = American Express

CB = Carte Blanche

DC = Diners Club

MC = MasterCard

V = Visa

Important: All rates are the most recent available but are subject to change. Check with the inn before making reservations.

Captain Mey's Inn, 38; rates: $40 to $60 dbl. BB; MC, V
Casselman Inn, 19; rates: $20 to $38.50 dbl. EP
Cedar Hill, 111; rates: $50 dbl. BB
Centre Bridge Inn, 182; rates: $50 to $85 dbl. EP
Century Inn, 199; rates: $40 dbl. EP
Chalfonte Hotel, 39; rates: $64 to $96 dbl. MAP; MC, V
Chequit Inn, 143; rates: from $40 dbl. EP (MAP available); AE, DC, MC, V
Chestnut Hill, 53; rates: $45 dbl. BB
Cliff Park Inn, 178; rates: $55 to $70 per person dbl. oc. AP; AE, MC, V
Clinton House Restaurant and Inn, 86; rates $35 to $40 dbl. EP; AE, MC, V
Cobblestones, 109; rates on request; EP
Colgate Inn, 116; rates: $38 to $50 dbl. EP; MC, V
Cooper Inn, 88; rates: $52 to $56 dbl. EP; AE, MC, V
Corner Cupboard Inn, 2; rates: $90 to $110 dbl. MAP (less off season); AE, MC, V
Country Inn, 203; rates: $30 to $60 dbl. EP; AE, MC, V
Coventry Forge Inn, 162; rates: from $35 dbl. BB
Depuy Canal House (and Brodhead House), 118; rates: $40 dbl. BB
Evermay-on-the-Delaware, 165; rates: $45 to $70 dbl. BB; MC, V
Fairfield Inn and Guest House, 169; rates: $35 dbl. EP; MC, V
Garnet Hill Lodge, 132; rates: $30 to $35 per person MAP
General Lewis Motor Inn, 207; rates: $32 to $47 dbl. EP; AE, MC, V
General Sutter Inn, 175; rates: $42 to $48 dbl. EP, suites higher; AE, MC, V
Genesee Falls Inn and Motel, 133; rates: $17 to $30 dbl. EP
Gingerbread House, 41; rates: $28 to $65 dbl. BB
Glen Iris Inn, 77; rates on request
Golden Eagle Inn, 107; rates: $50 to $75 dbl. BB; AE
Golden Pheasant Inn, 166; rates: $40 dbl. EP
Greenville Arms, 114; rates: $45 to $60 dbl. EP
Greystone Motor Lodge, 157; rates on request; AE, MC, V
Hedges House, 97; rates: $75 to $110 dbl. BB (less off season); AE, CB, DC, MC, V
Hedges on Blue Mountain Lake, 69; rates: $80 to $90 dbl. MAP
Hemlock Hall, 71; rates: $72 dbl. MAP (less off season)
Heritage Inn, 123; rates on request; AE, MC, V
Hickory Grove Inn, 90; rates: $22 to $34 dbl. BB; AE, MC, V
Horned Dorset Inn, 125; rates: $50 to $75 dbl. BB
Hostellerie Bressane, 121; rates: $45 to $75 dbl. BB
Hotel Bethlehem, 155; rates: $63 to $78 dbl. EP; AE, CB, DC, MC, V
Hotel du Village, 183; rates: $43 to $58 dbl. BB; AE
House on the Hill, 119; rates: $45 to $55 dbl. BB
Hudson House, 87; rates: $45 to $65 dbl. BB, suites higher; MC, V
Hulbert House, 72; rates: $20 to $22 dbl. EP; MC, V
Huntting Inn, 99; rates: $50 to $75 dbl. EP; AE, DC, MC, V
Inn at Belhurst Castle, 110; rates: $75 dbl. BB; AE, DC, MC, V
Inn at Buckeystown, 11; rates: $65 to $85 dbl. MAP
Inn at Mitchell House, 13; rates: $60 to $70 dbl. BB; MC, V
Inn at Perry Cabin, 27; rates: $80 to $120 BB; AE, MC, V
Inn at Phillips Mill, 184; rates: $44 dbl. EP
Inn at Quogue, 135; rates: $70 to $100 dbl. BB; AE, MC, V
Inn at Starlight Lake, 201; rates: $35 to $50 per person MAP; MC, V
Inn at the Shaker Mill, 75; rates: $30 to $35 per person BB, $62.50 AP
Inn on the Library Lawn, 152; rates: from $45 dbl. EP; AE, DC, MC, V
Innisfree, 195; rates: $55 to $76 dbl. EP
Kalorama Guest House, 4; rates $40 to $45 dbl. BB
Kittle House, 128; rates: $60 dbl. EP; AE, DC, MC, V
Lambertville House, 51; rates: $30 to $50 dbl. EP; AE, MC, V
Logan Inn, 185; rates: $50 to $60 dbl. EP; MC, V
Maidstone Arms, 100; rates: $35 to $90 dbl. BB; AE, MC, V
Mainstay Inn, 42; rates: $42 to $62 dbl. BB

THE COMPLEAT TRAVELER'S READER REPORT

To: *The Compleat Traveler*
    c/o Burt Franklin & Co., Inc.
    235 East 44th Street
    New York, New York 10017 U.S.A.

Dear Compleat Traveler:

I have used your book in _____ (country or region).
I would like to offer the following ☐ new recommendation, ☐ comment,
☐ suggestion, ☐ criticism, ☐ or complaint about:

Name of Country Inn or Hotel:

_____

Address: _____

_____

Comments:

Day of my visit: _____   Length of stay: _____

From (name): _____

Address _____

_____ Telephone: _____